AF264521

THE THREAD OF HIS LOVE

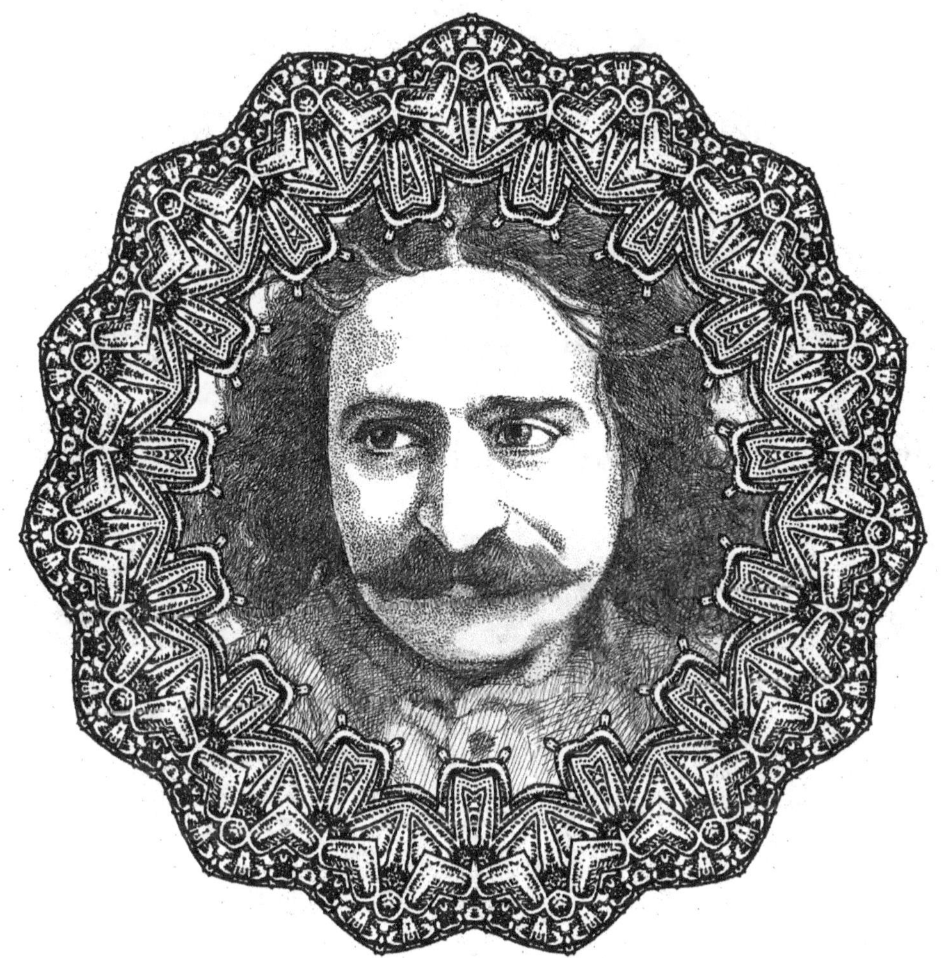

MANDALAS AND HAIKU

KARL MOELLER AND IRMA SHEPPARD

Acknowledgements & Copyright

Haiku copyright © Irma Sheppard 2020

Mandala art copyright © Karl Moeller 2020

Cover portrait of Avatar Meher Baba © Claire Mataira

Font Book Antiqua

ISBN 978-0-578-67871-9

Other books by Irma Sheppard:

Where Love Could Take Me
Inheritance
The Well of Longing

Irma Sheppard as Editor and Compiler:

101 Tales of Finding Love, Vols. 1,2 and 3
Meher Baba's Samadhi: Tales From the Beloved's Tomb

Other books by Karl Moeller:

Return to Treasure Island
Among the Sleeping: Sufism Within and Without Islam

This book of haiku is dedicated to Avatar Meher Baba, the Source of
all love and inspiration.

Irma Sheppard
April 2020

I've drawn much of my life, and got in the habit of saving the better images.
These mandalas are created from original, usually abstract, pen and ink
pieces.

It was a fascinating process pairing mandala with haiku.

I hope you enjoy this nearly as much as we did making it.

Karl Moeller
Asheville NC
2020

Slowly, steadily
He speaks to the heart of my
Being—*I am here.*

There is no Real way
to describe Love — it comes from
no place but His Grace.

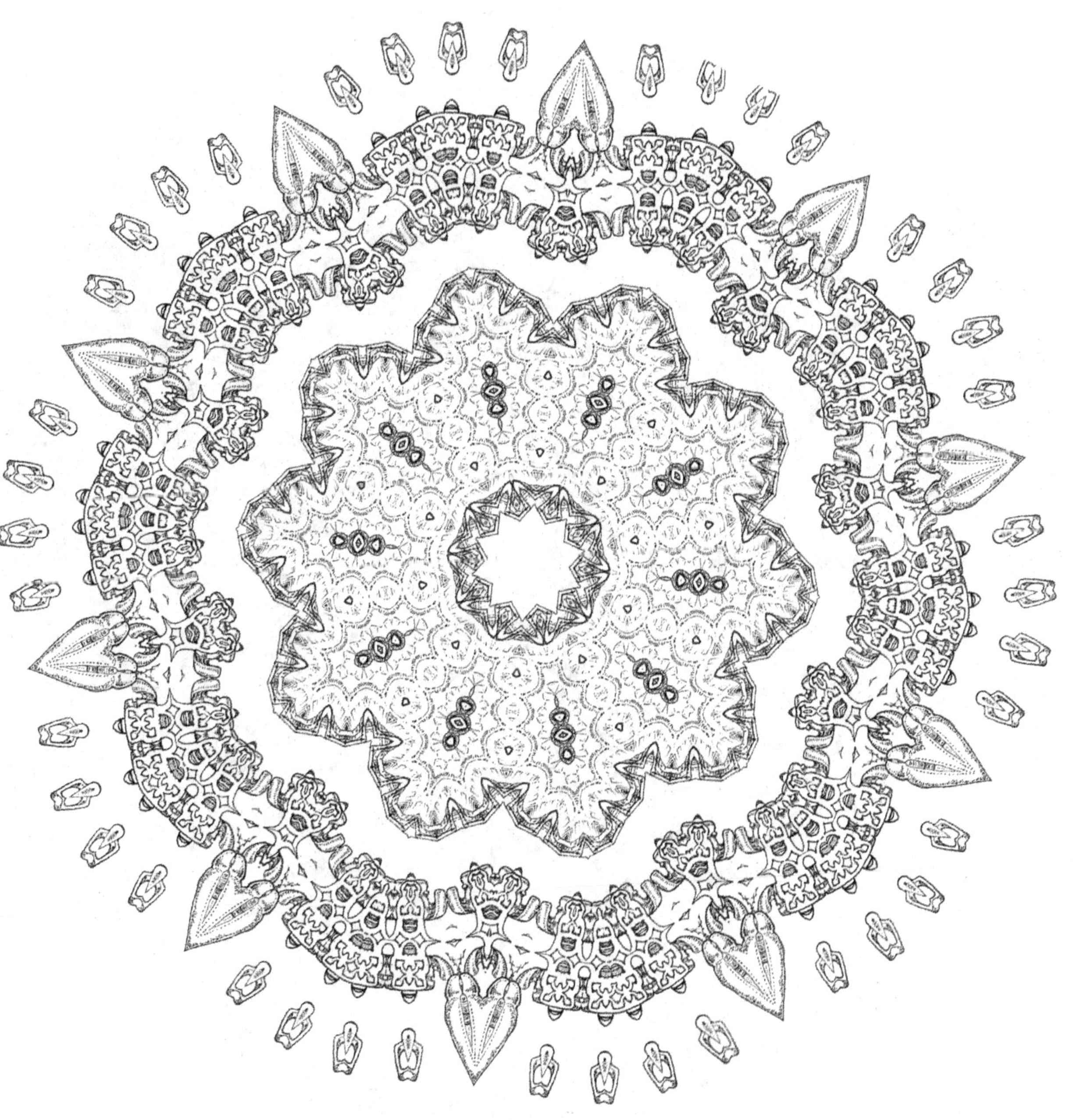

Your eyes of kindness
unveil me. Who am I? I am
You, but not just yet.

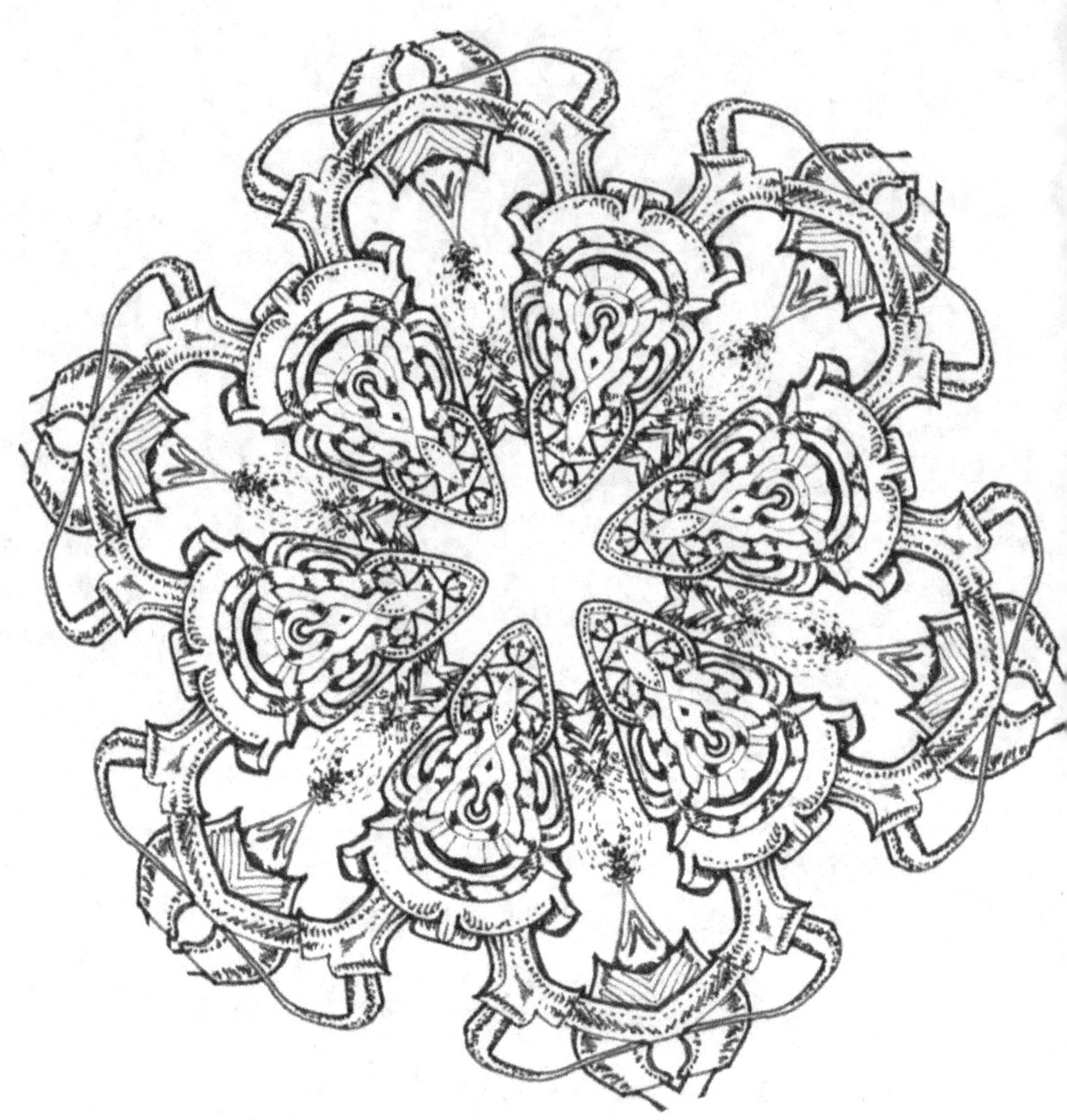

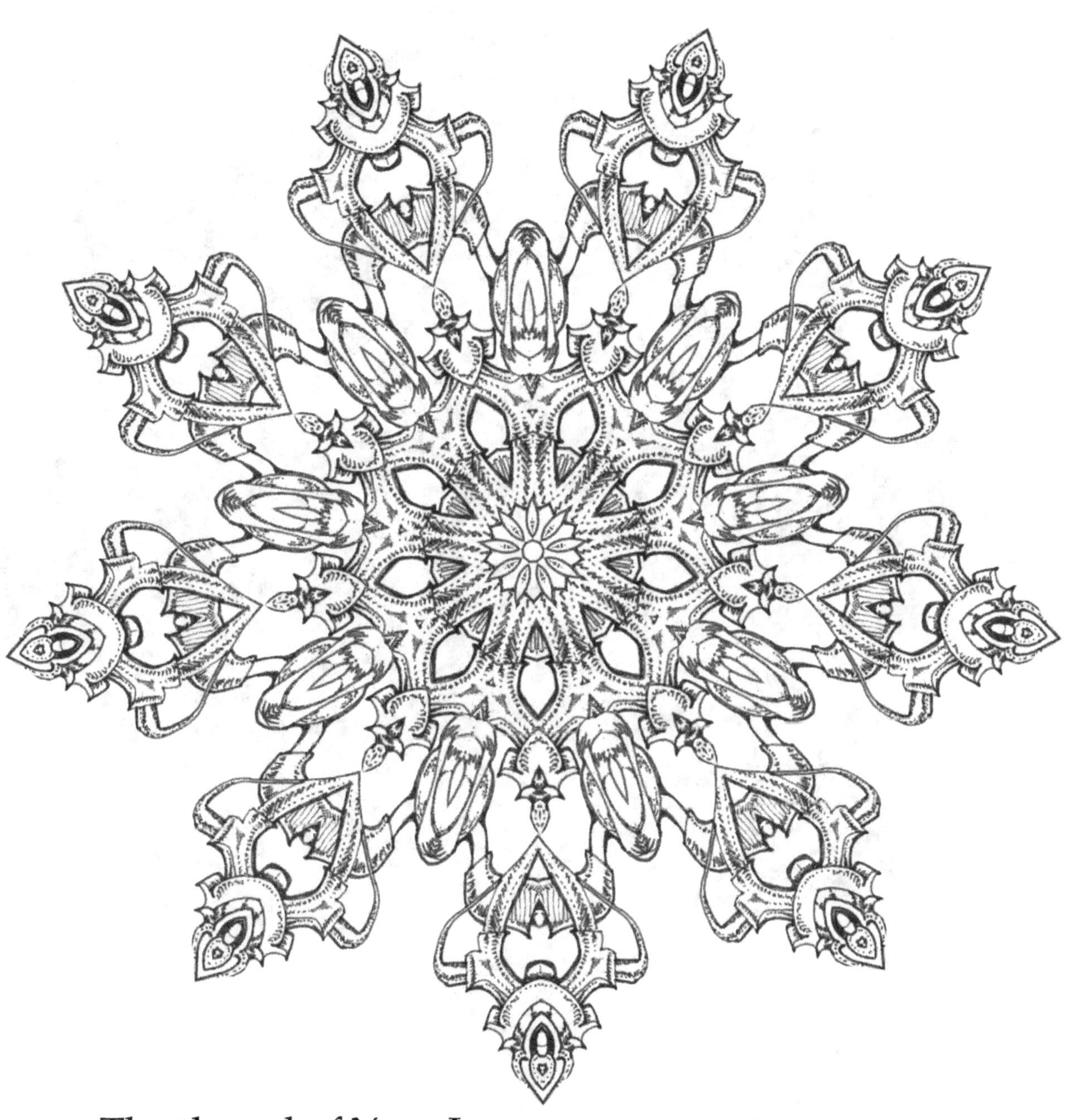

The thread of Your Love
draws me safely through the eye
of Maya's needle.

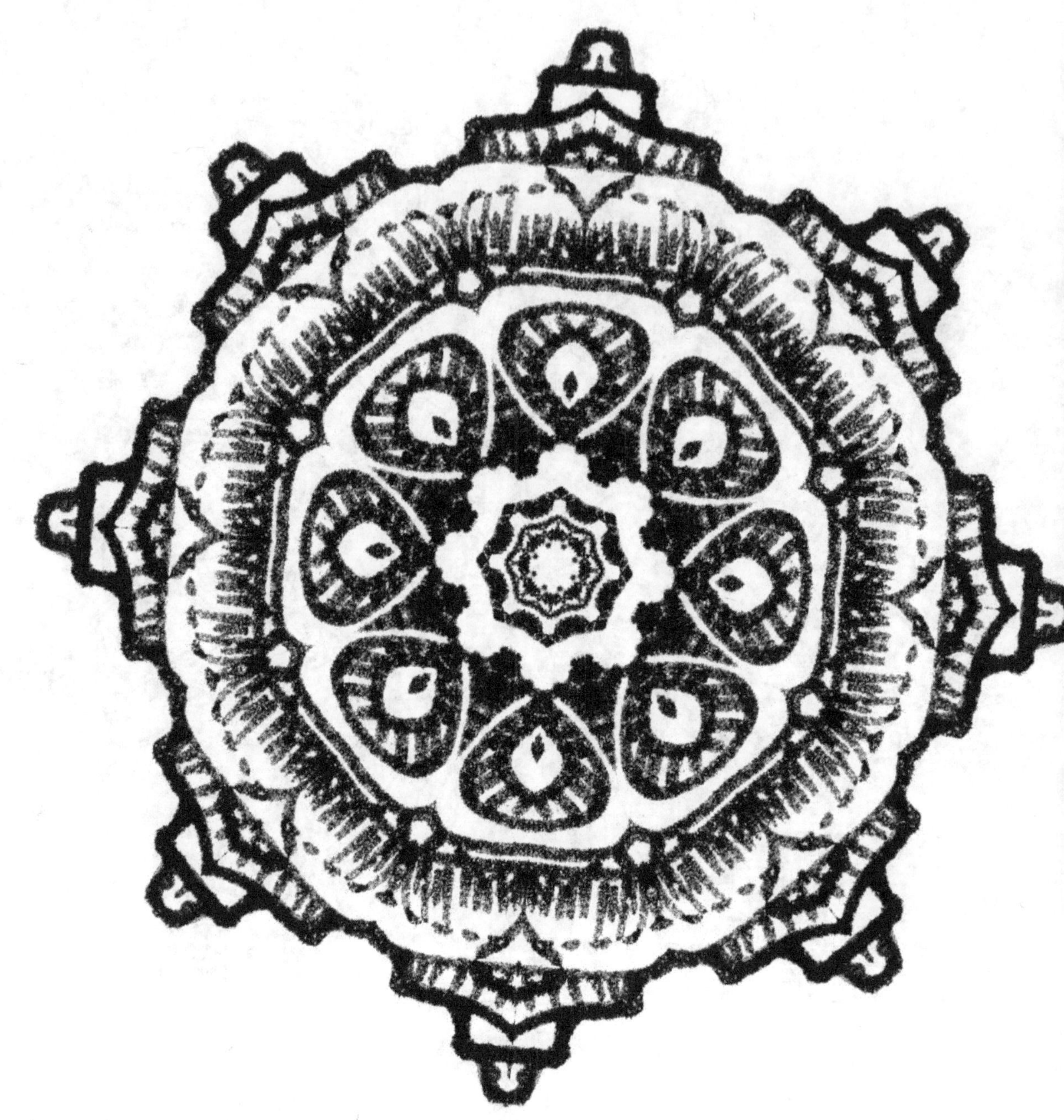

The glow in Your eyes—
drops of Reality rain
deeply into mine.

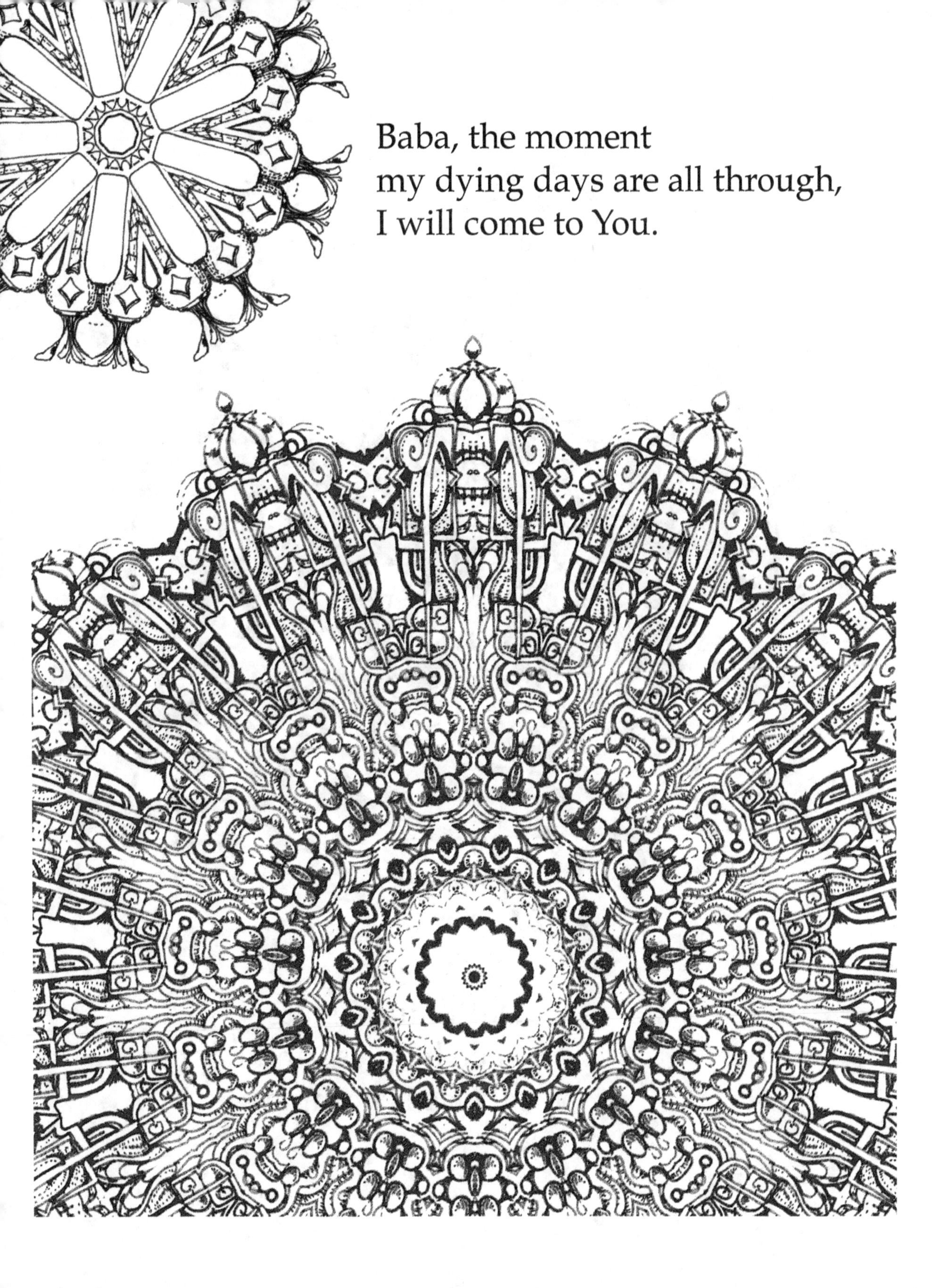

Baba, the moment
my dying days are all through,
I will come to You.

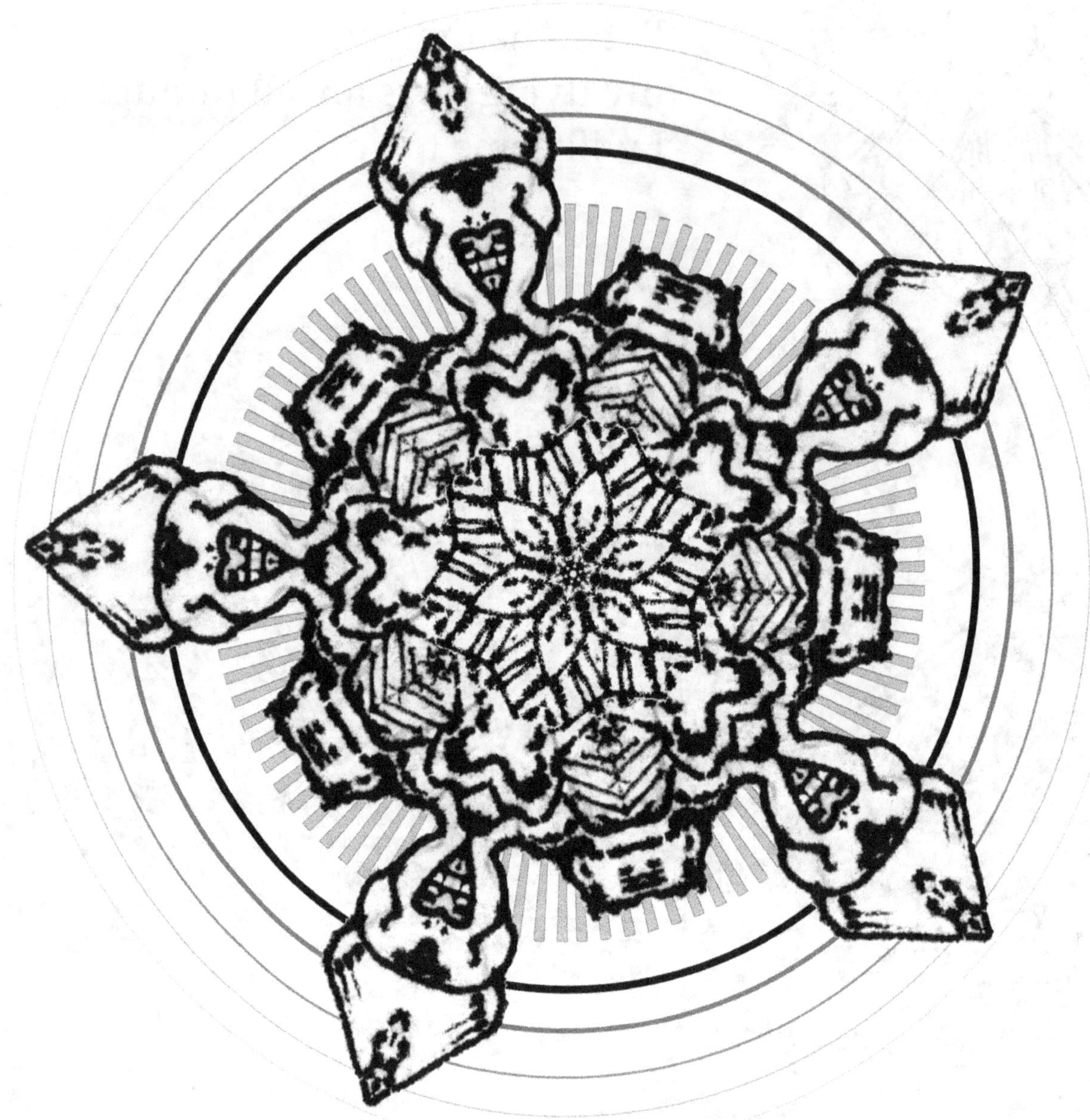

Our natural state —
to be helpless and hopeless —
all else is nothing.

I see You see me—
I know I'm in the Real place
inside my true Self.

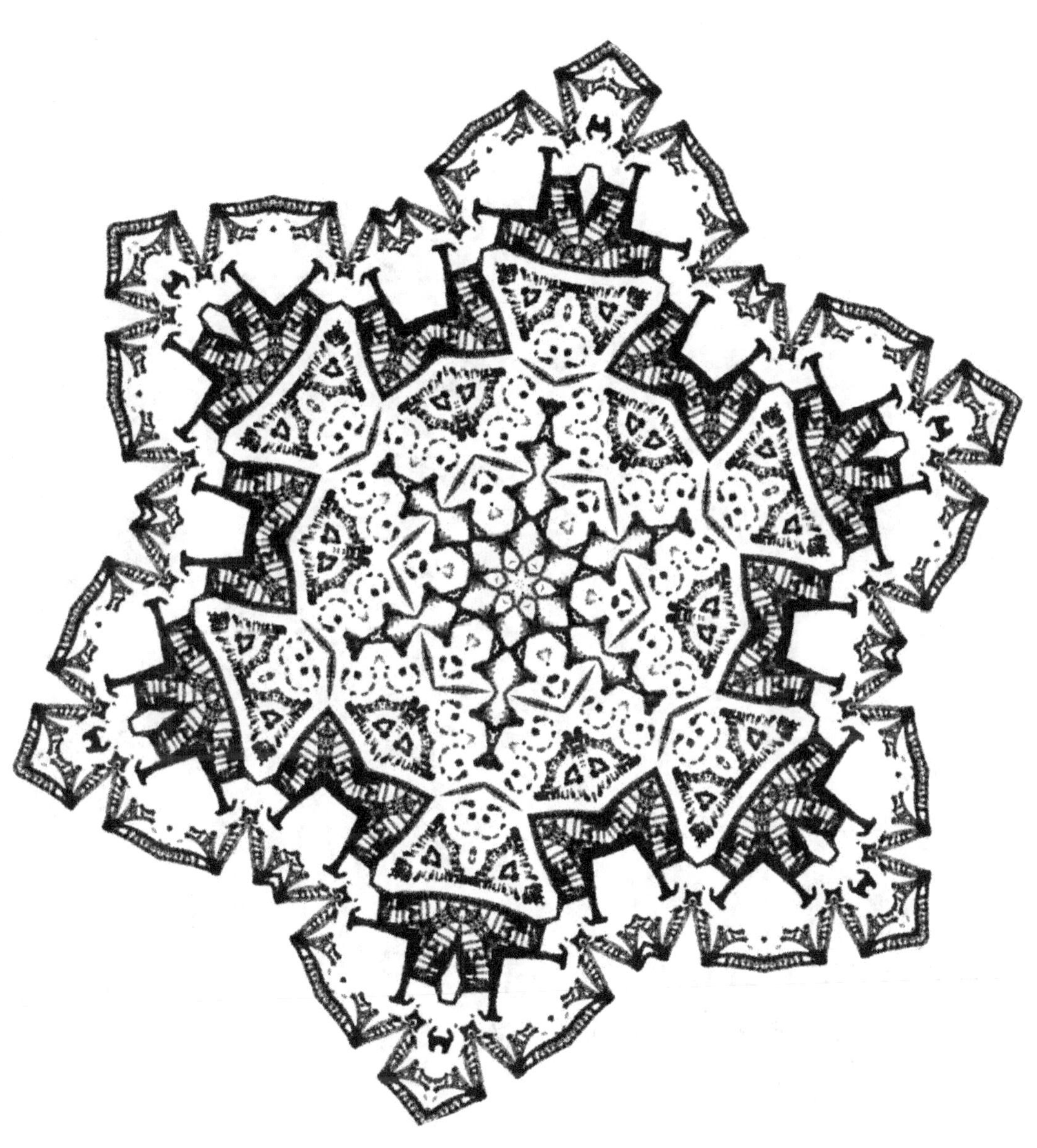

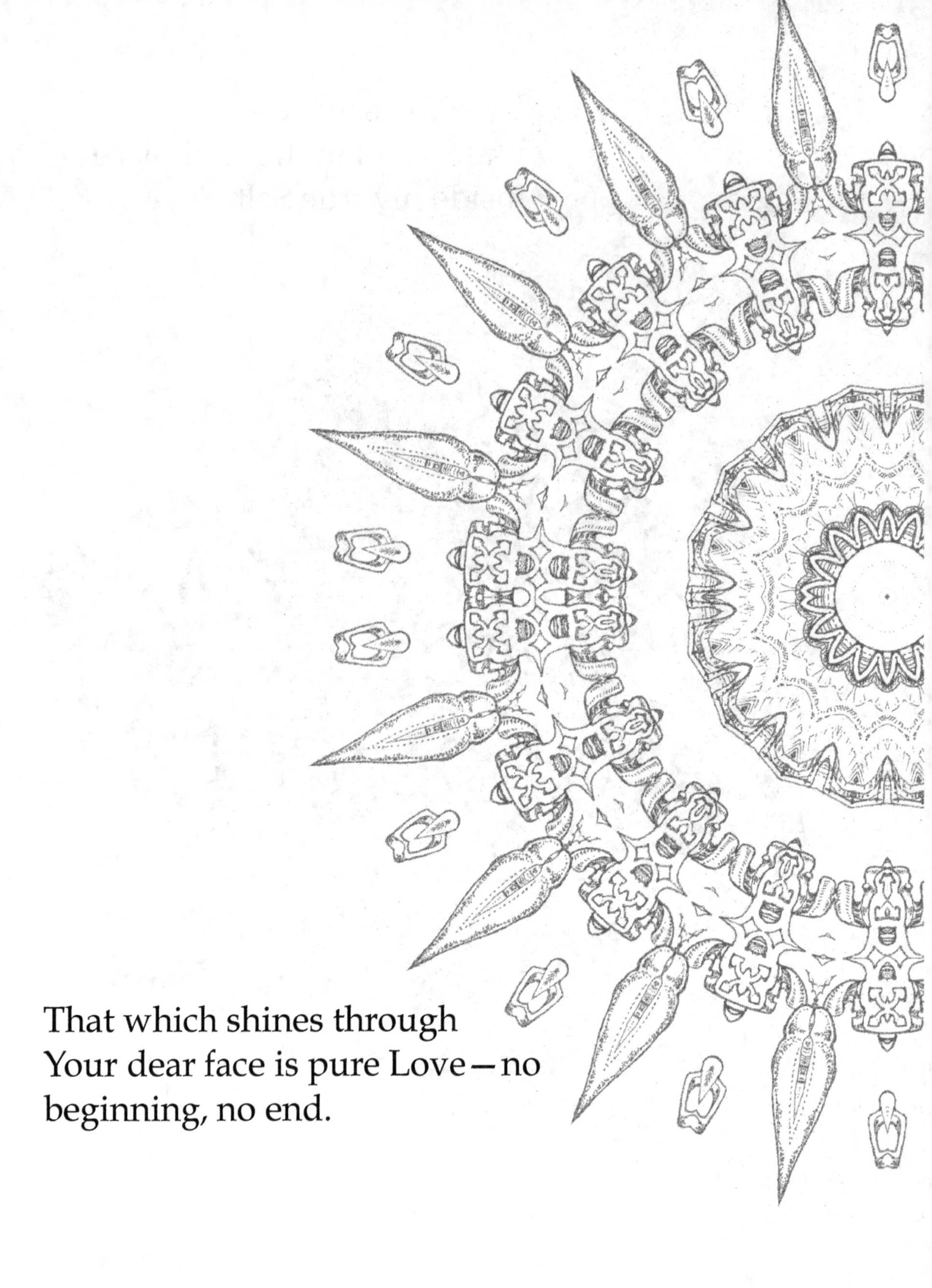

That which shines through
Your dear face is pure Love — no
beginning, no end.

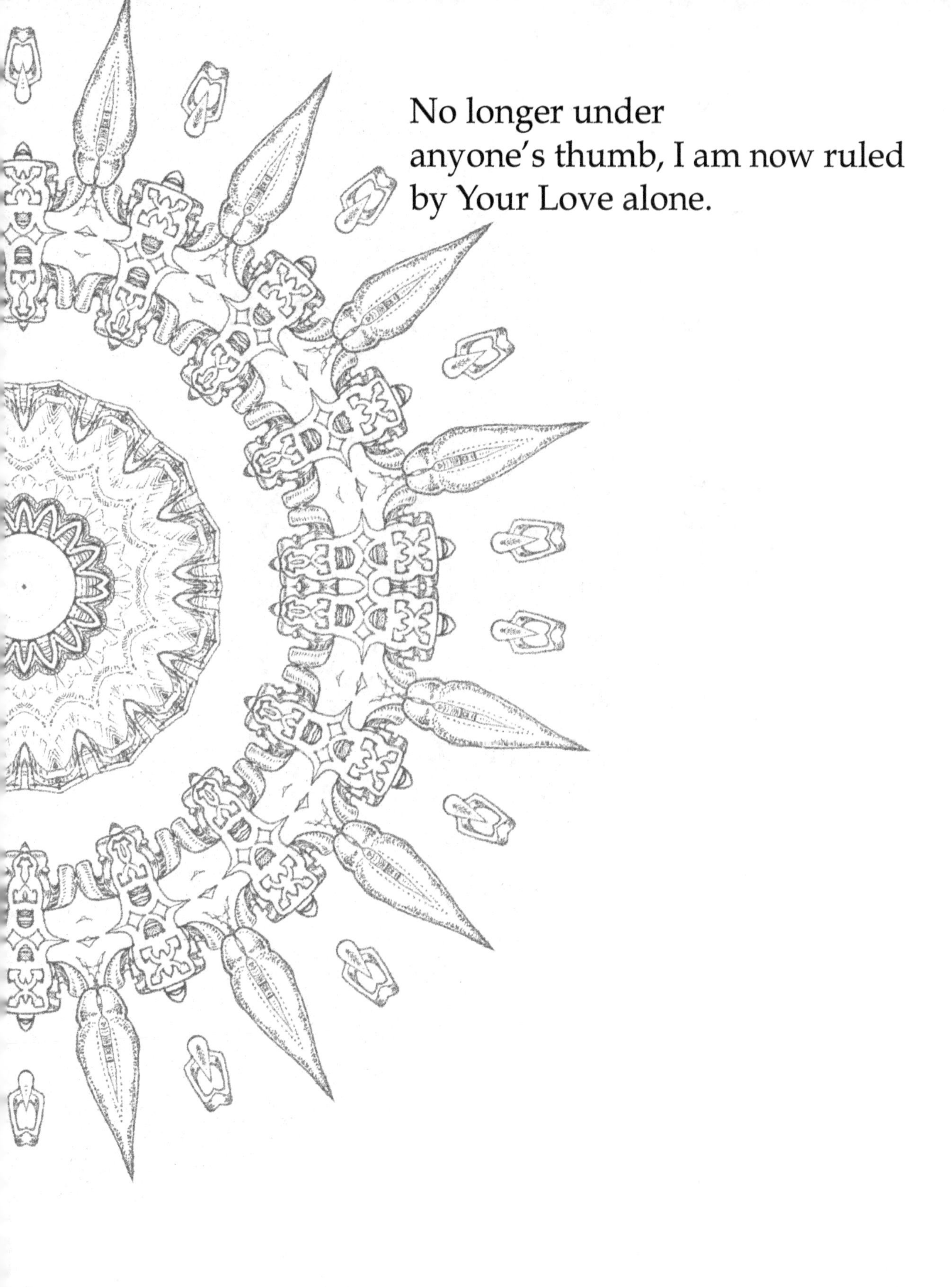

No longer under
anyone's thumb, I am now ruled
by Your Love alone.

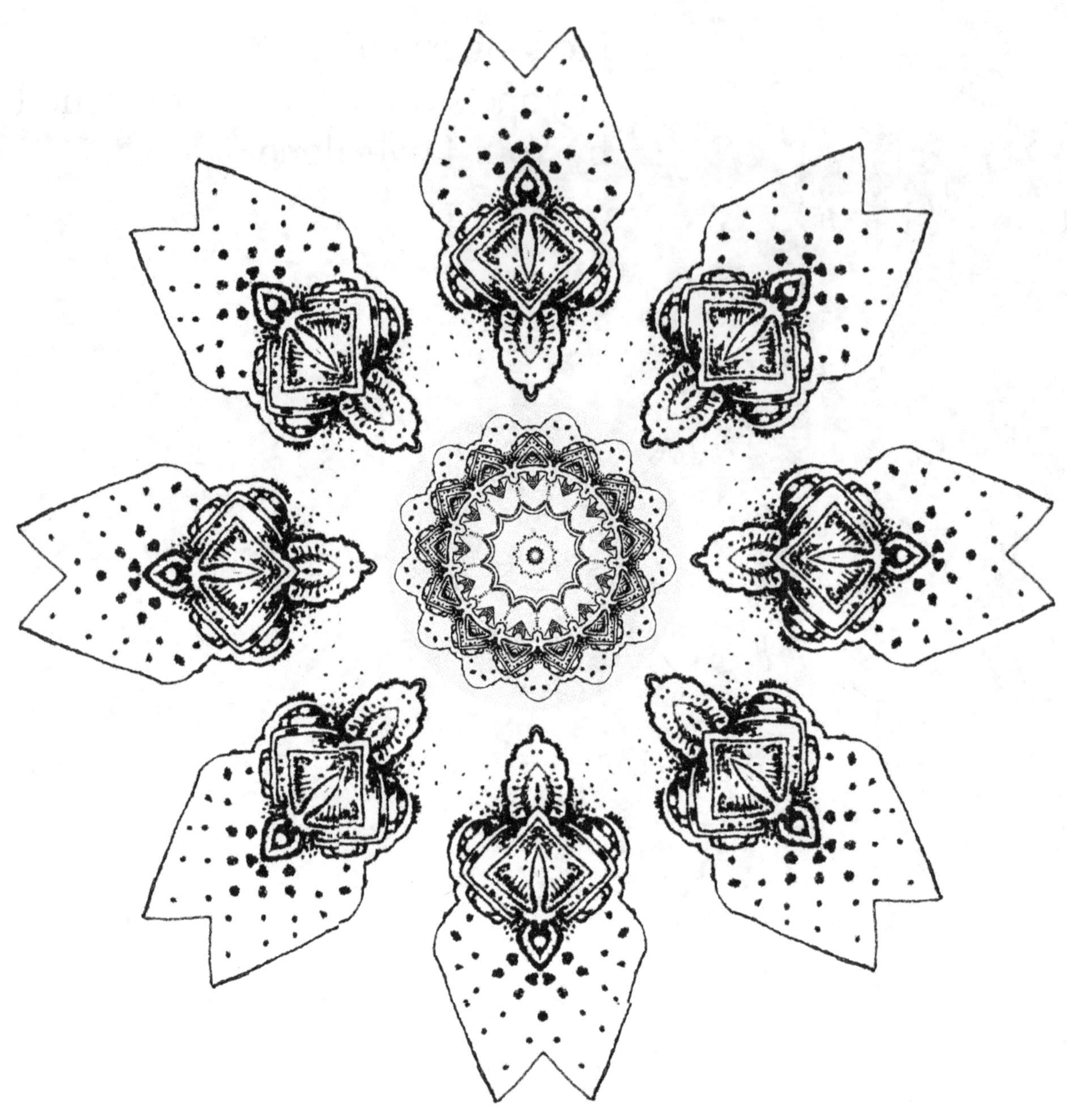

Many messages
in laughter — light, dark or grey.
Fly the highest plane.

Teatime, chocolate.
Water gentles down from the sky.
Earthly delights, oh my!

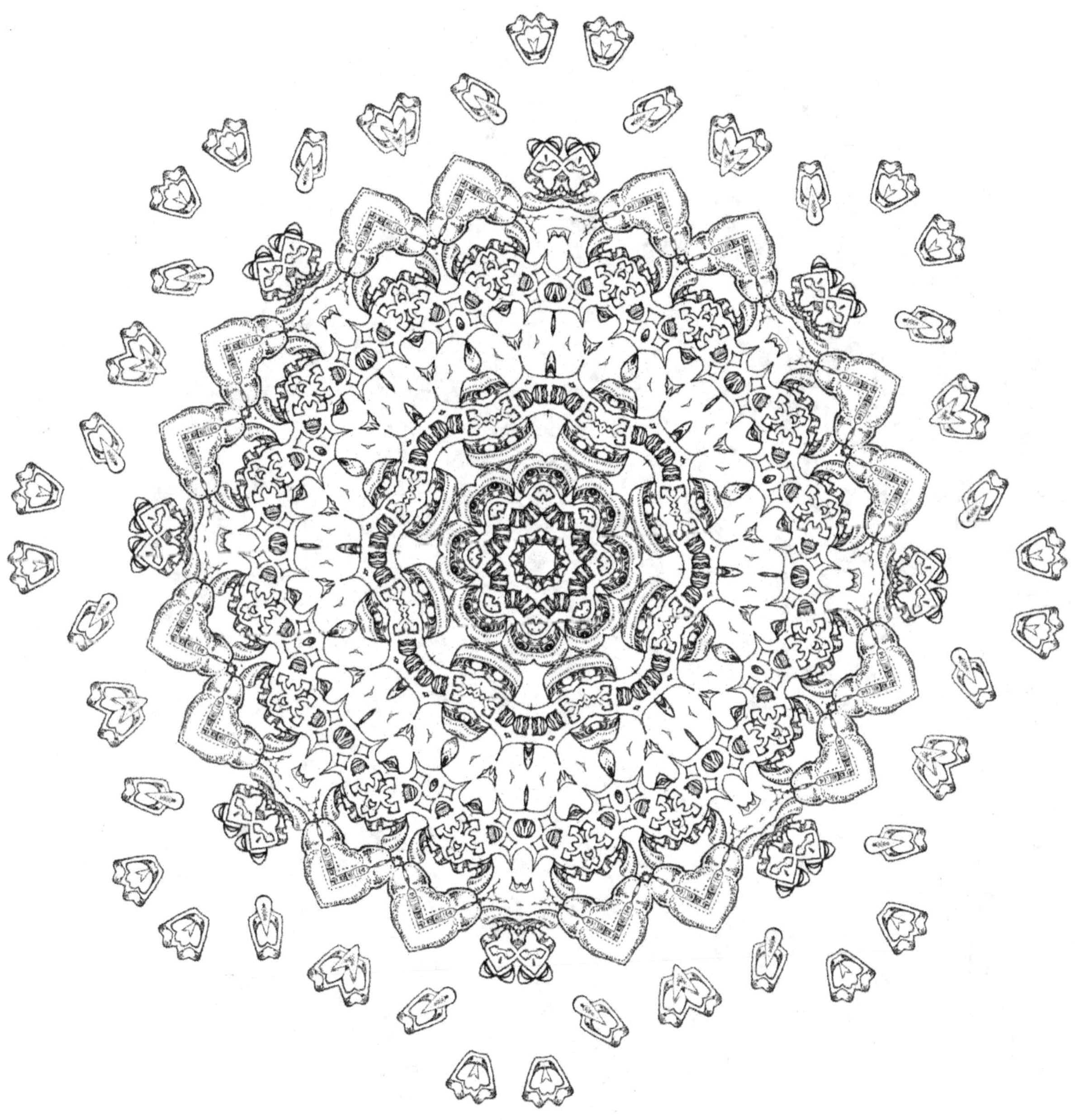

When I saw His face
I knew to follow this Man
anywhere, forever.

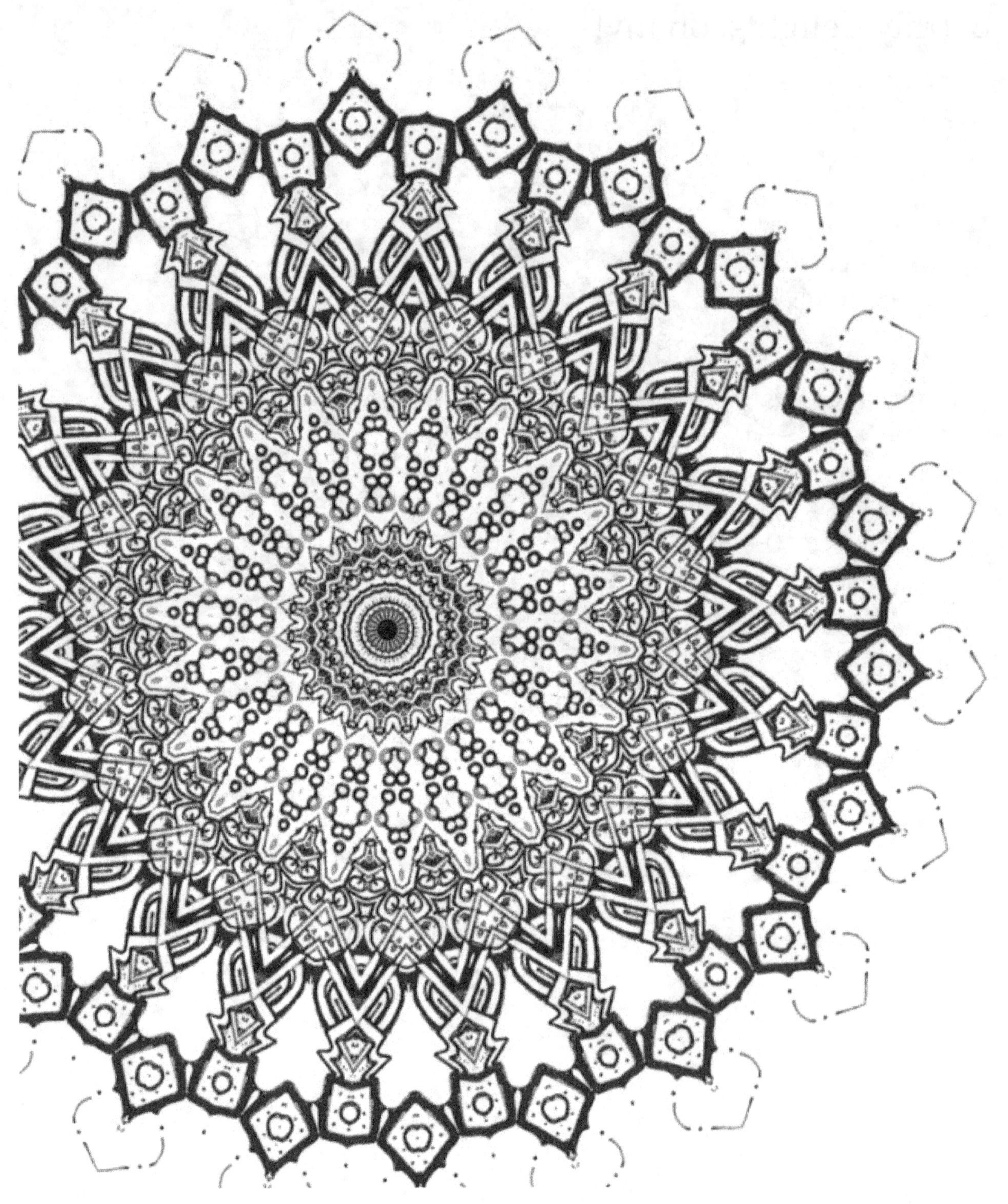

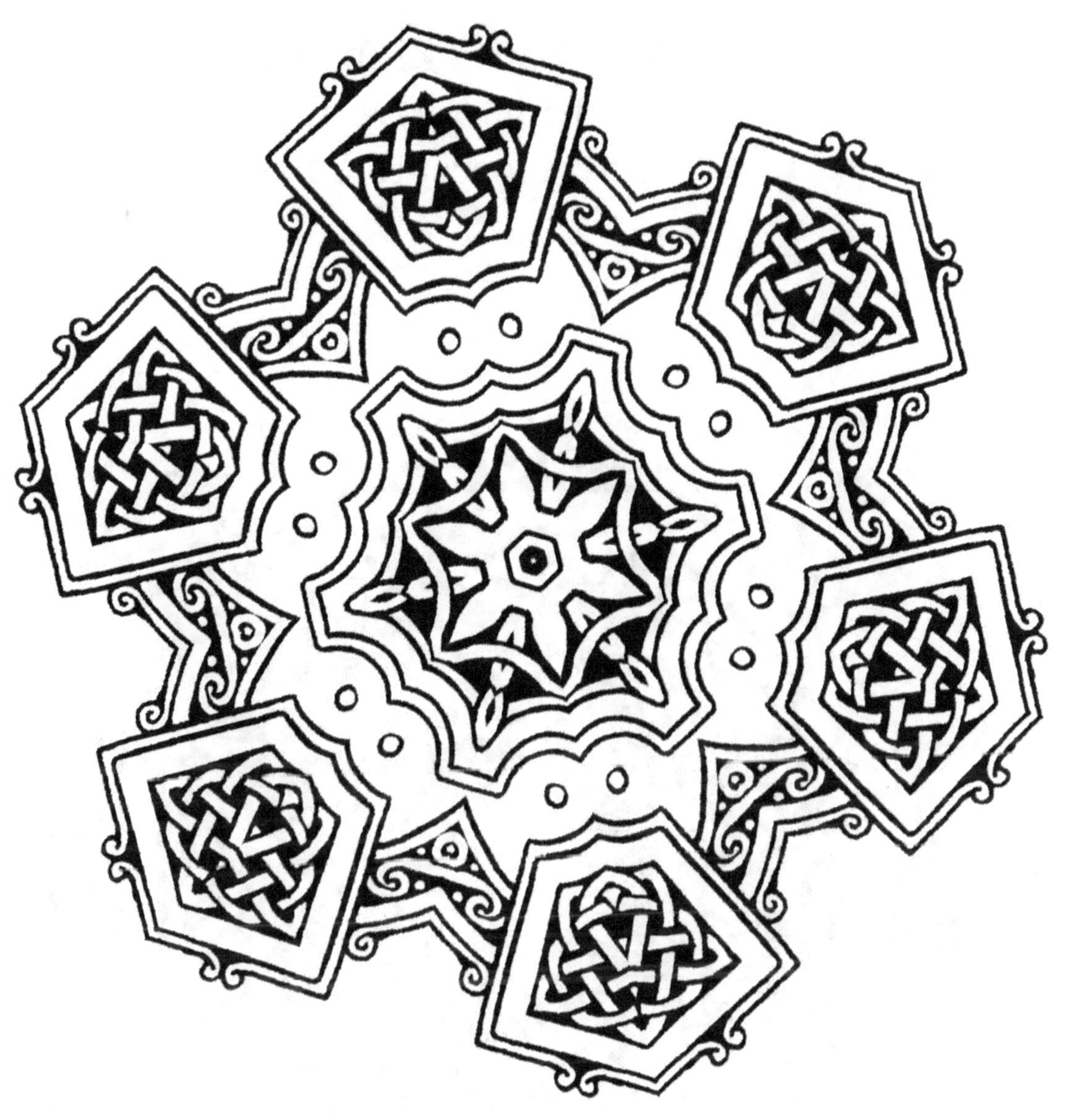

I waken within—
know the one value in life
is just to please You.

My desires keep You
far from me. Desireless, I
draw closest to You.

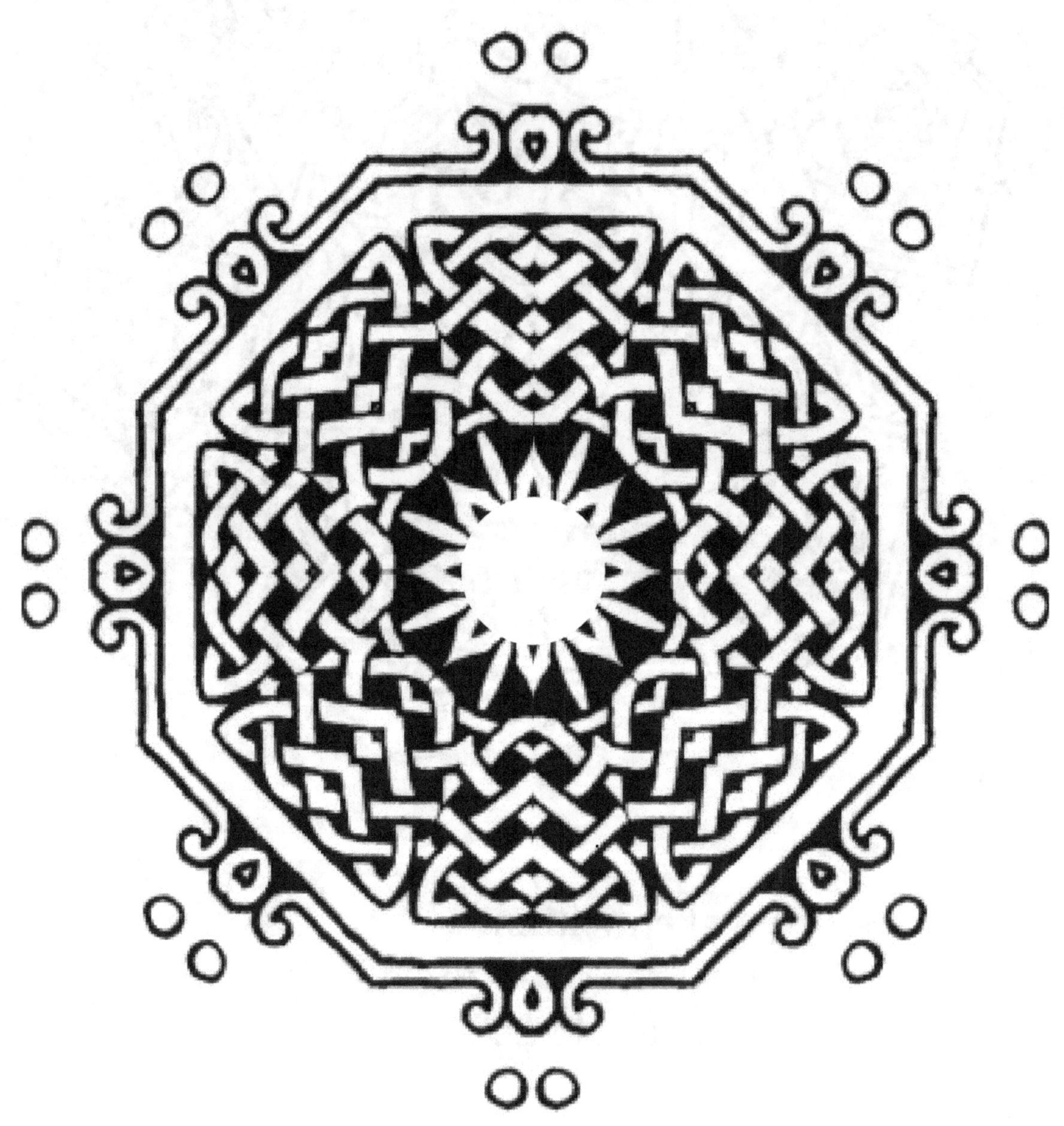

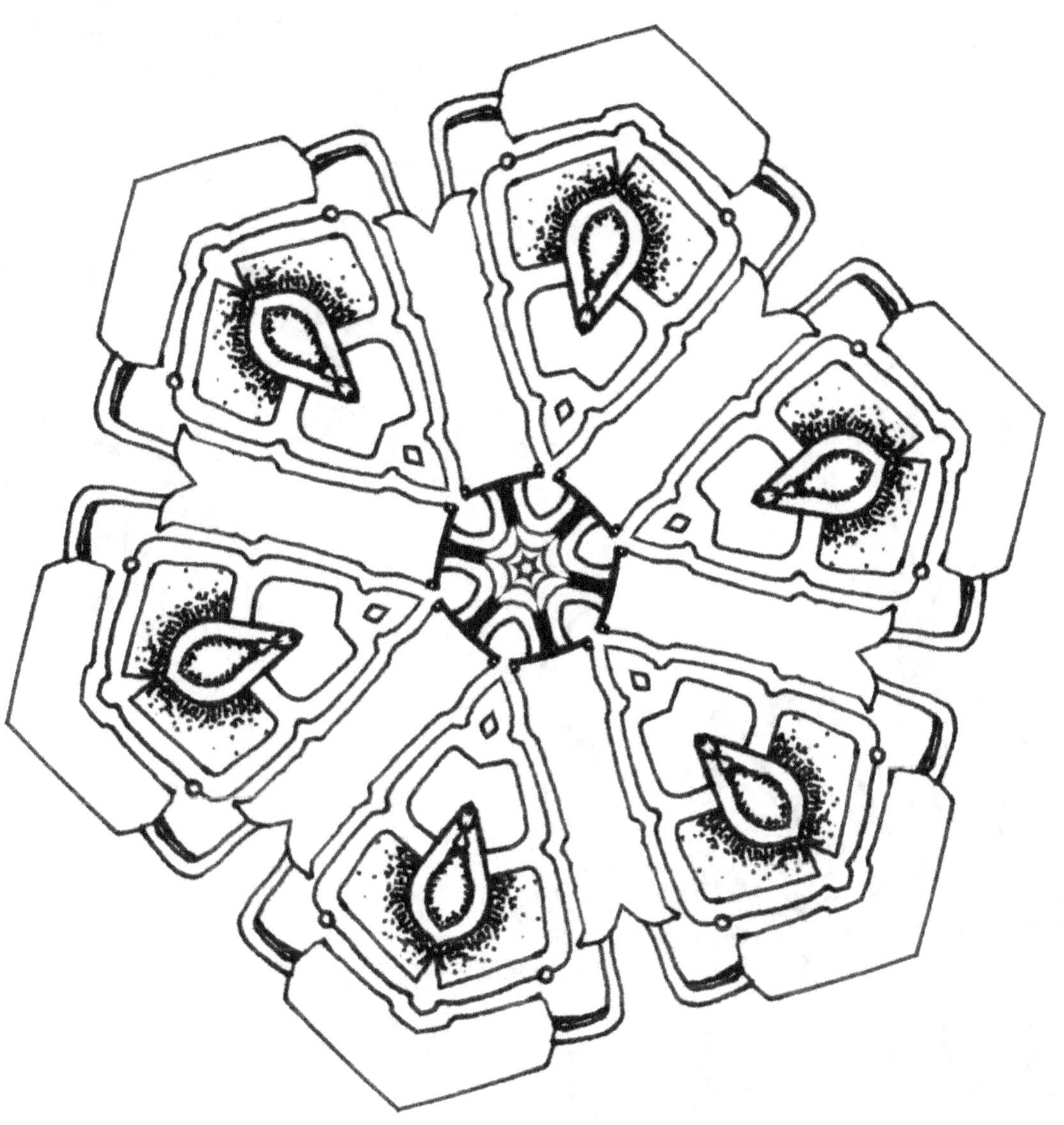

On the back burner
of His Love — not forgotten
but on hold — Hold on !

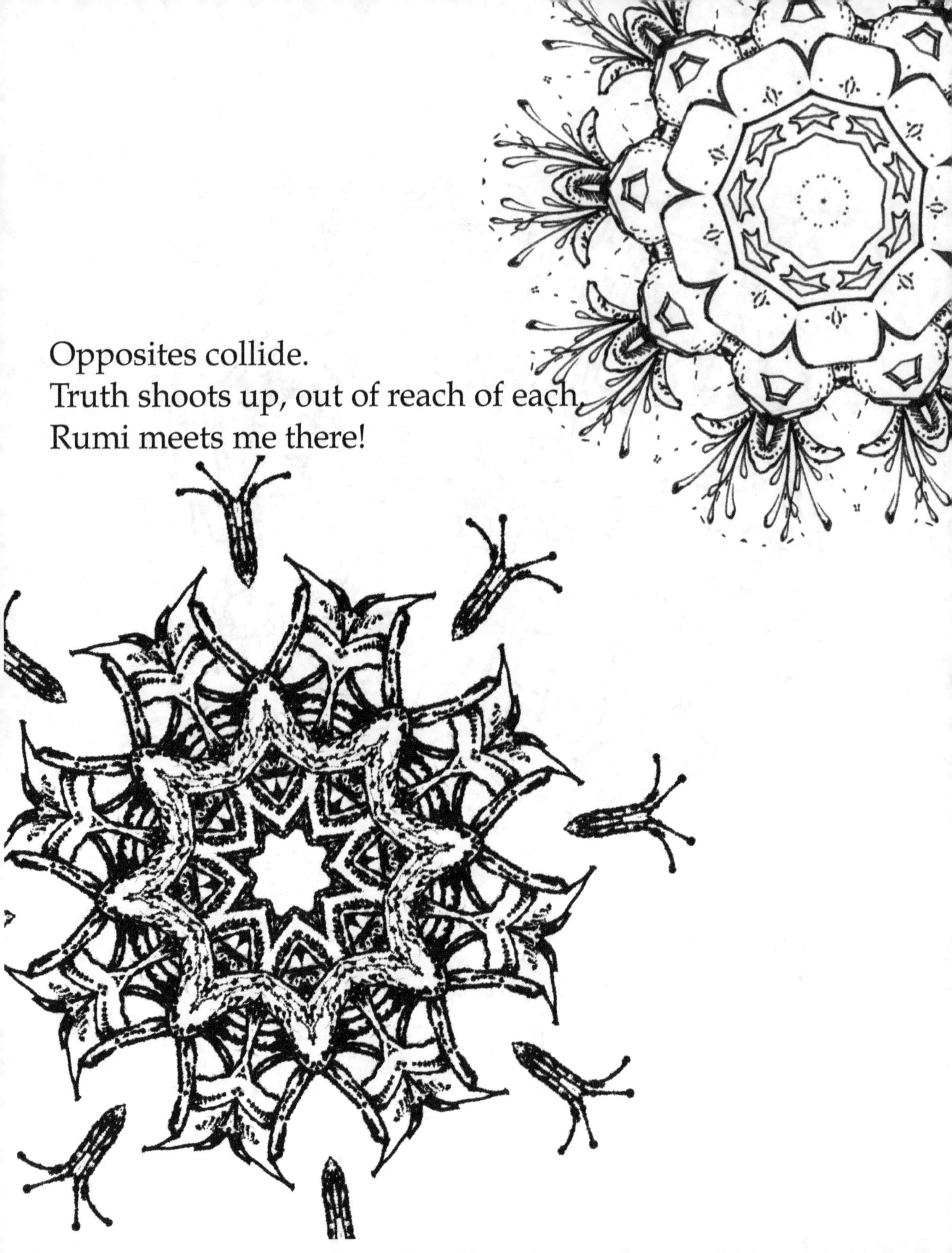

Opposites collide.
Truth shoots up, out of reach of each.
Rumi meets me there!

This side and that side—
Rumi's field—the only place
I am whole inside.

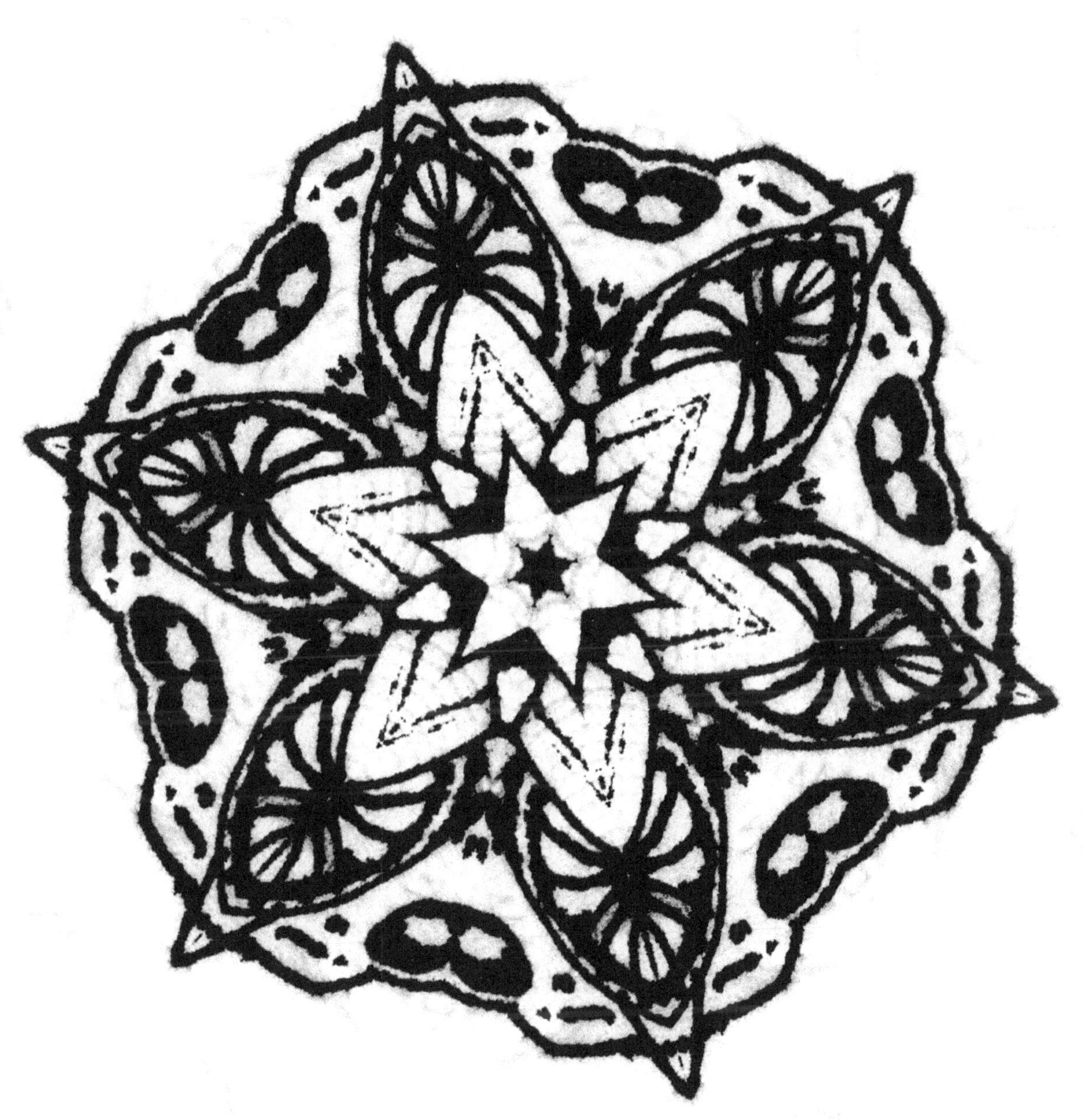

Dogwood petals float
white through forest greenery.
Bouquets of springtime.

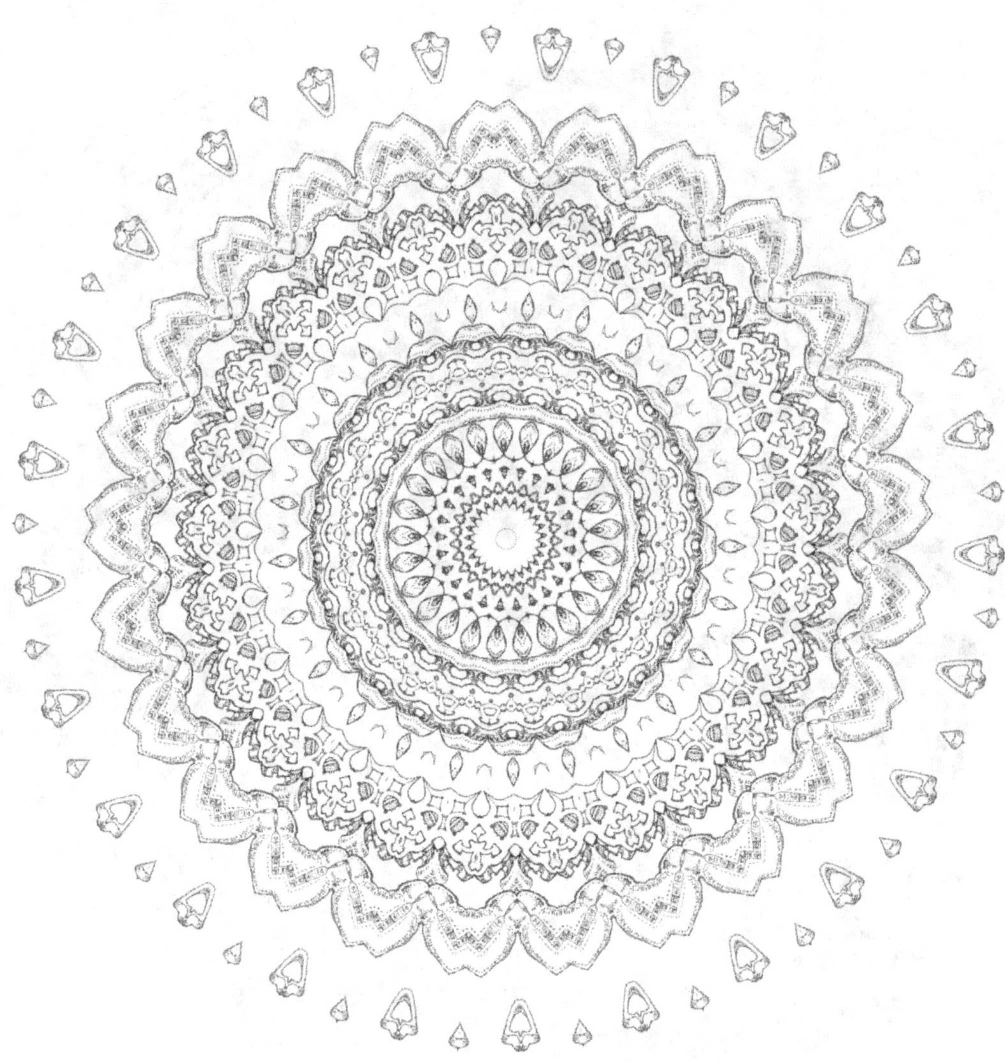

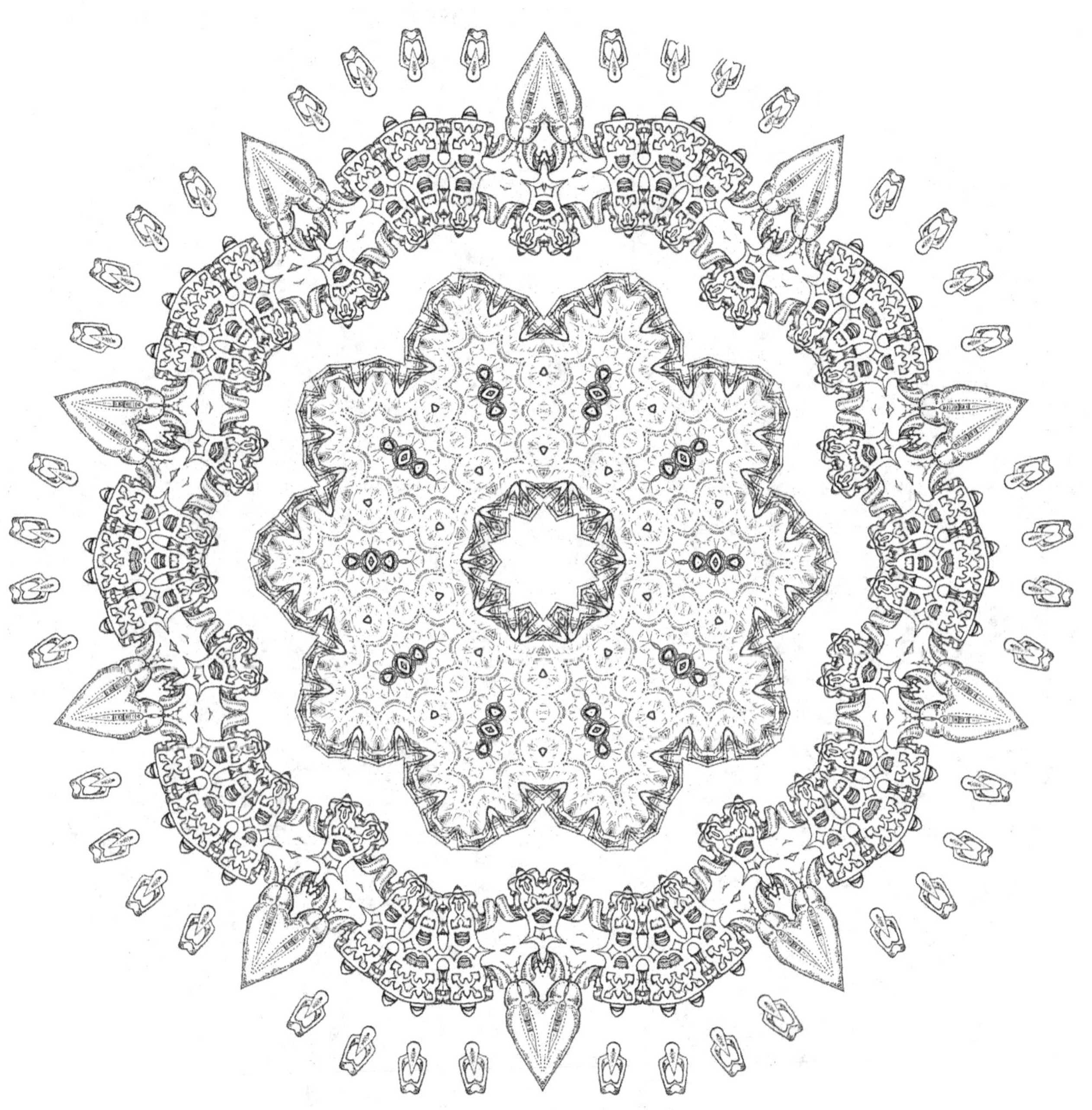

May — the land revels
in its brazen greenery.
Clouds gadding on high.

Quiet mind catches
the scented shadow of Your hair.
A wild blessedness.

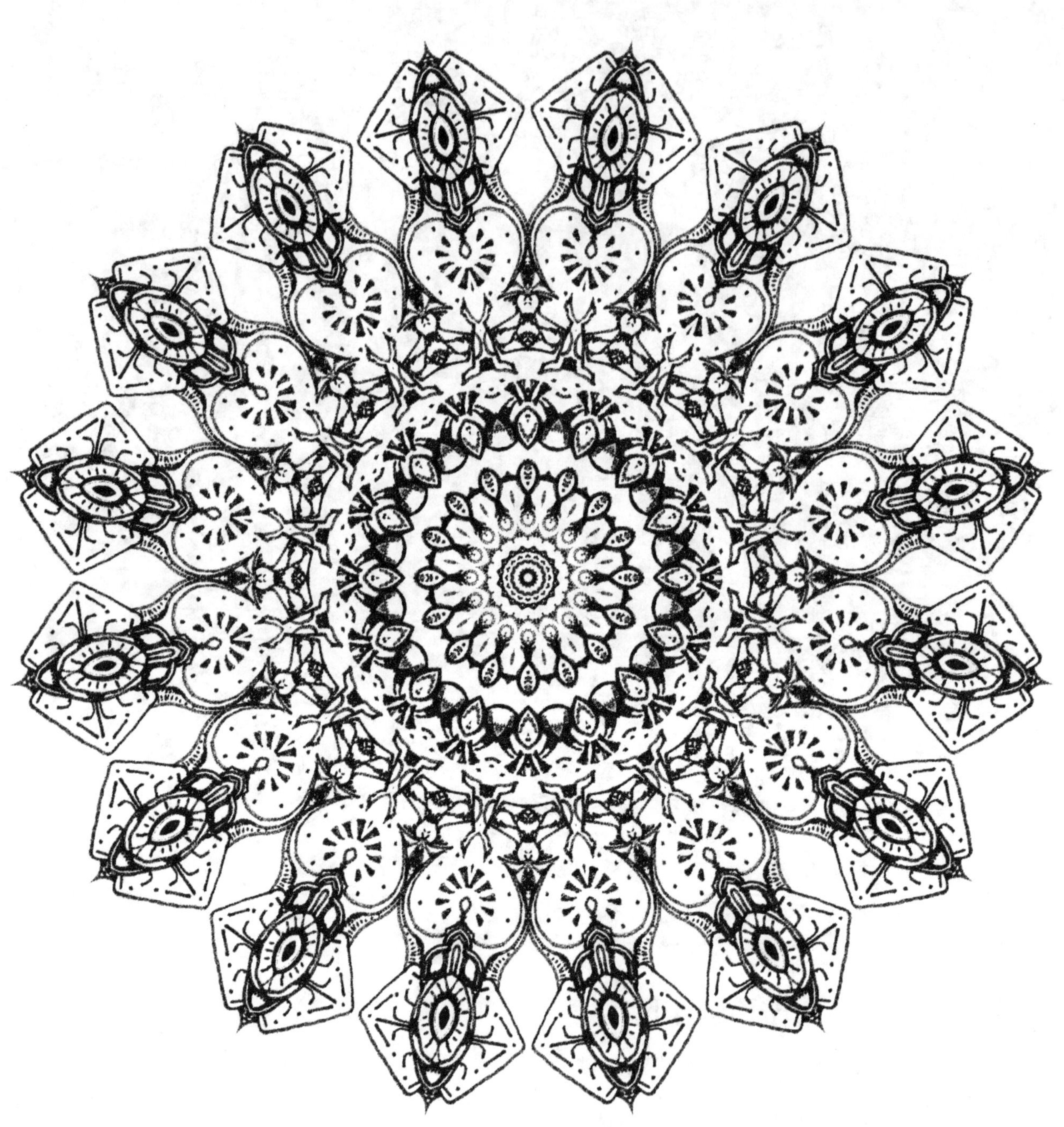

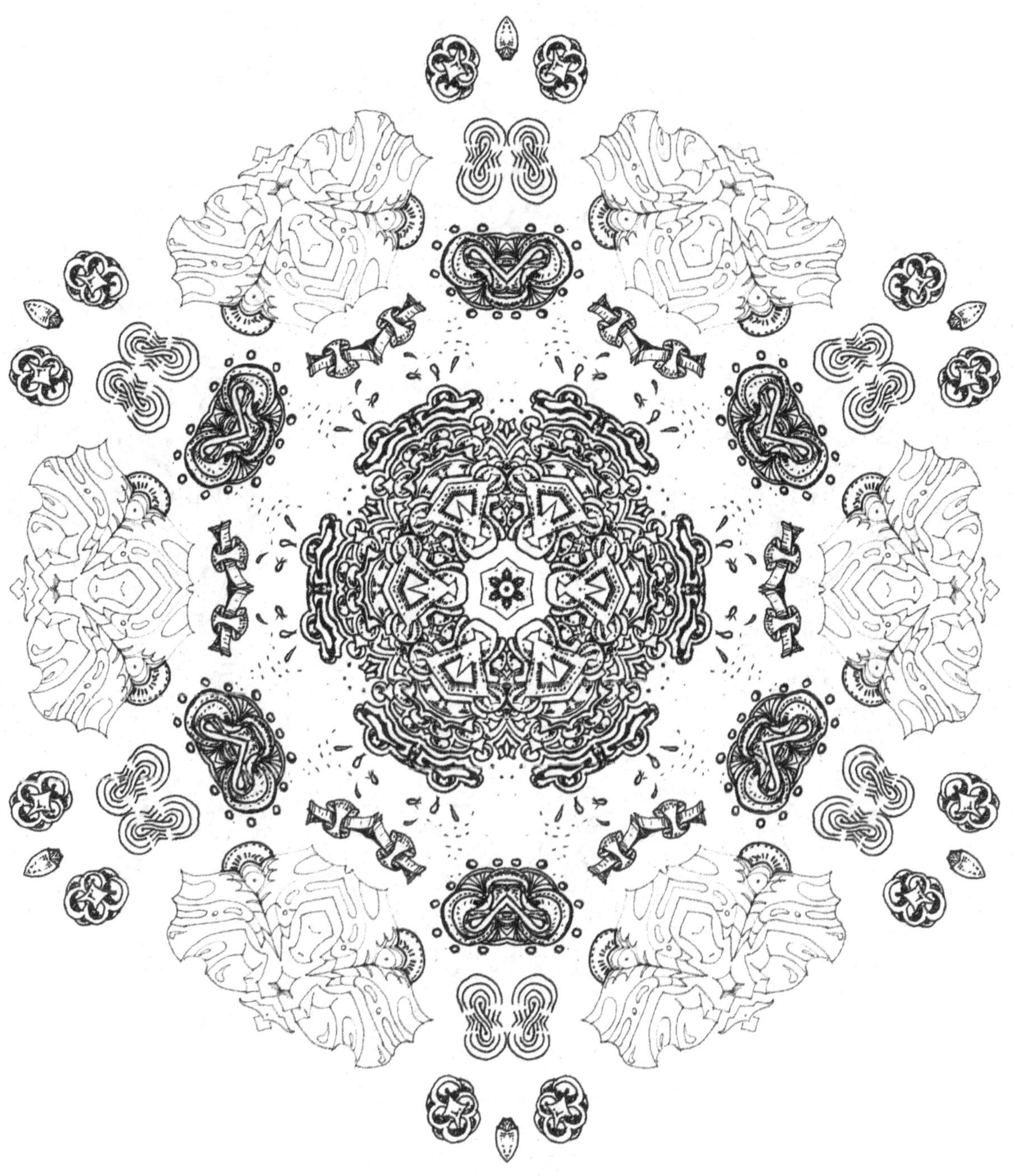

Questioning mind spins
as if planting cut flowers.
Crazed along its edges.

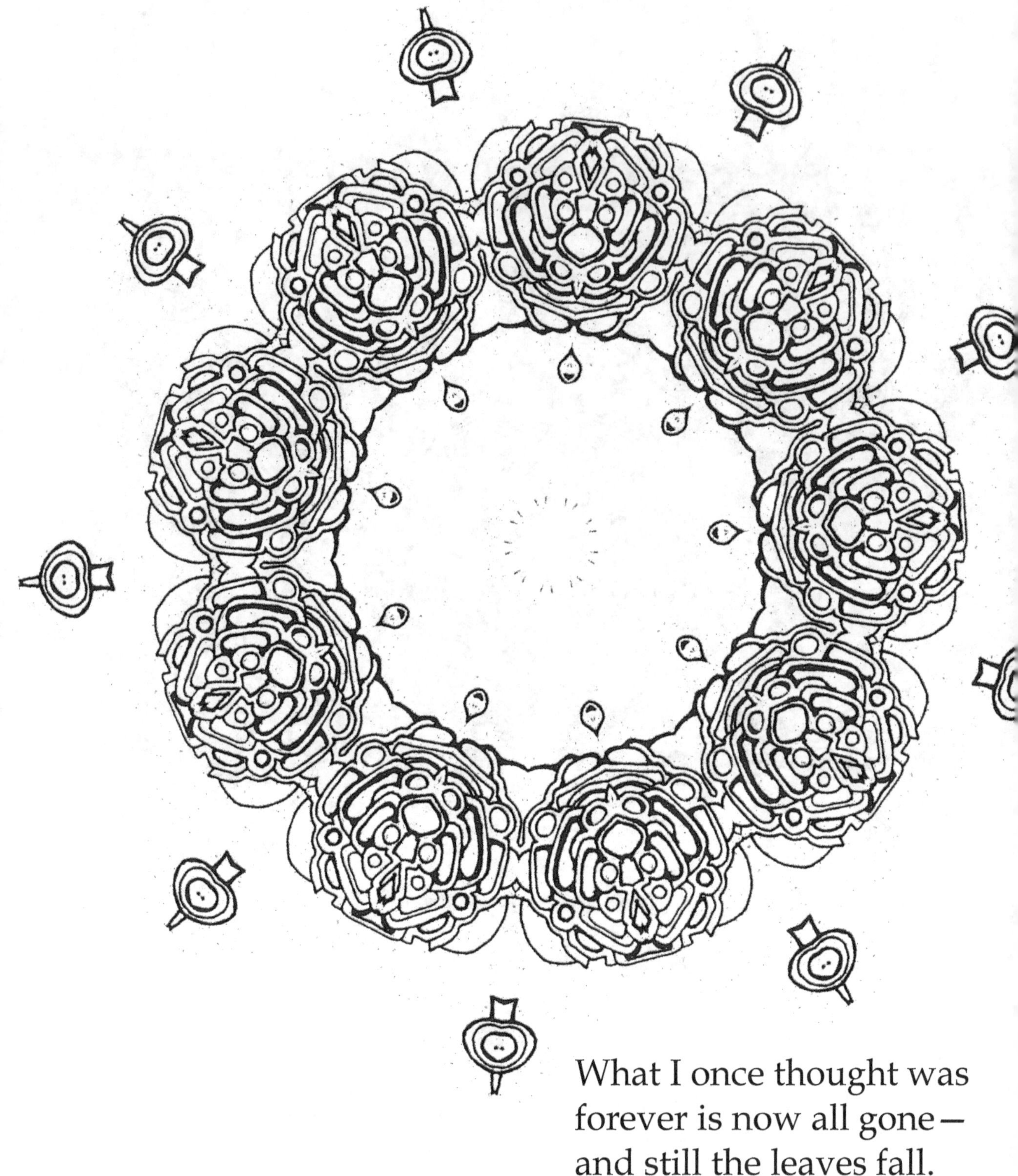

What I once thought was
forever is now all gone—
and still the leaves fall.

Challenge and opportunity—
to be present to Love's Beauty.
Forever is *Now!*

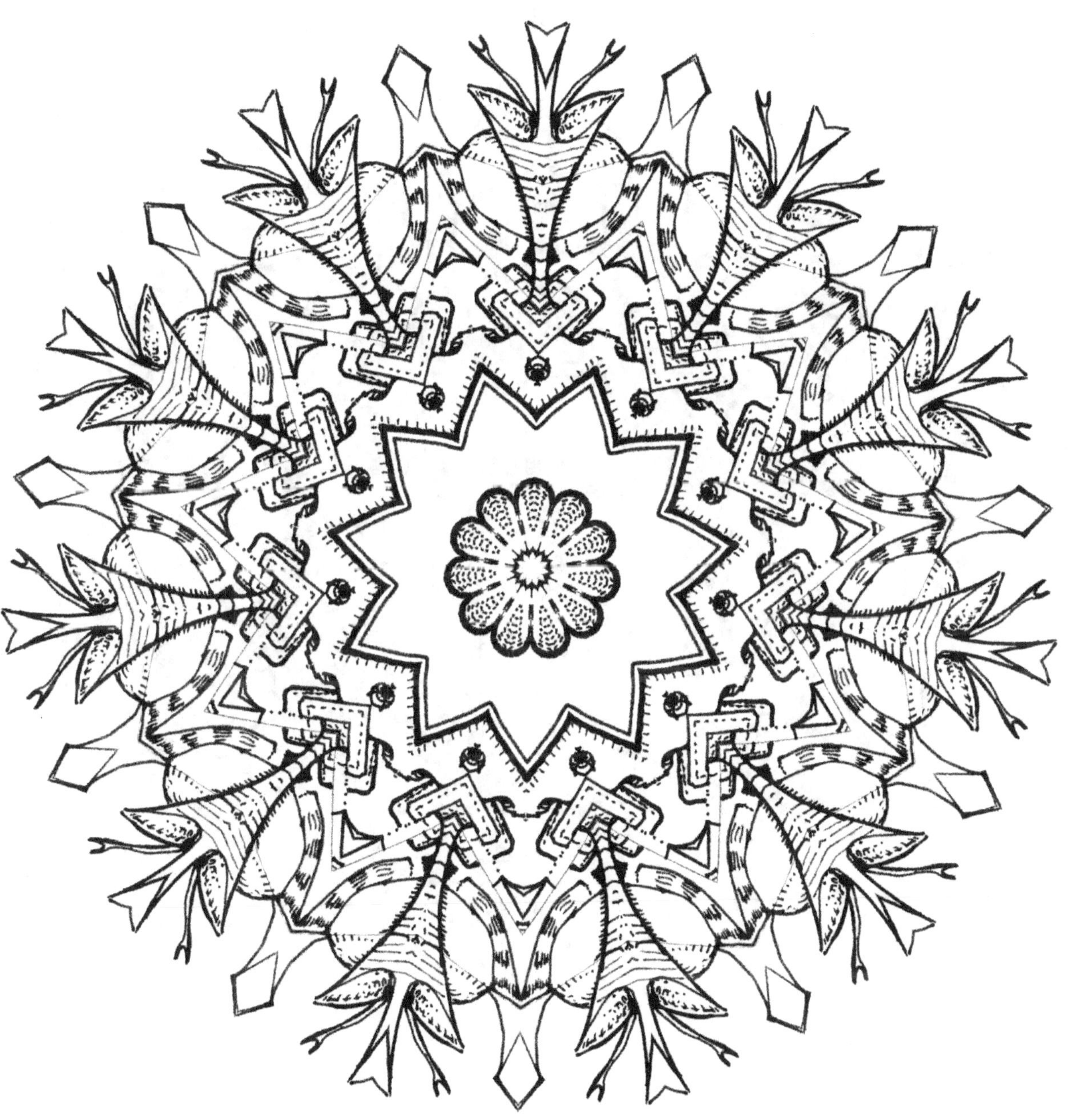

Baba came to true
standards of our lives—straight from
the White Horse's mouth.

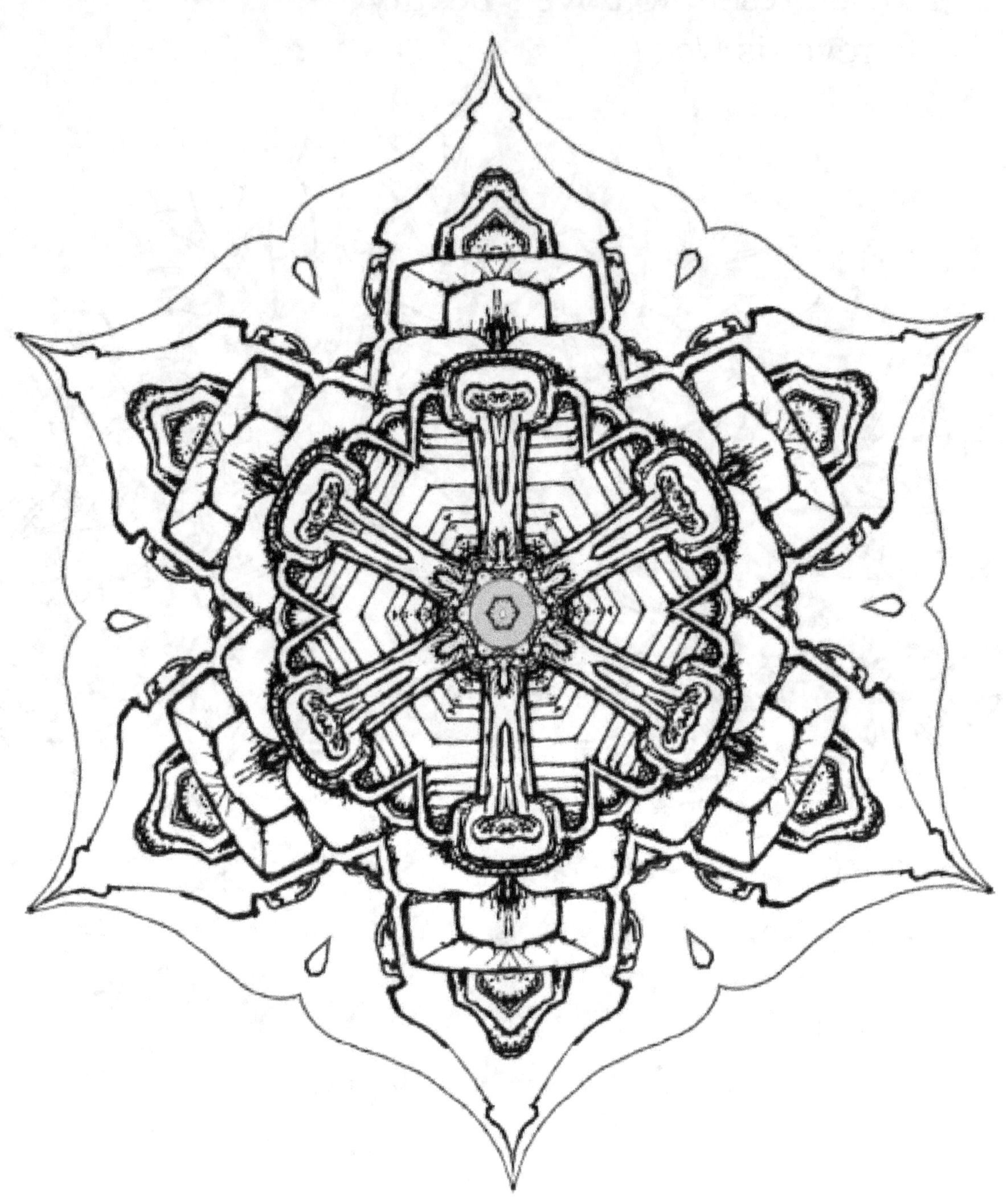

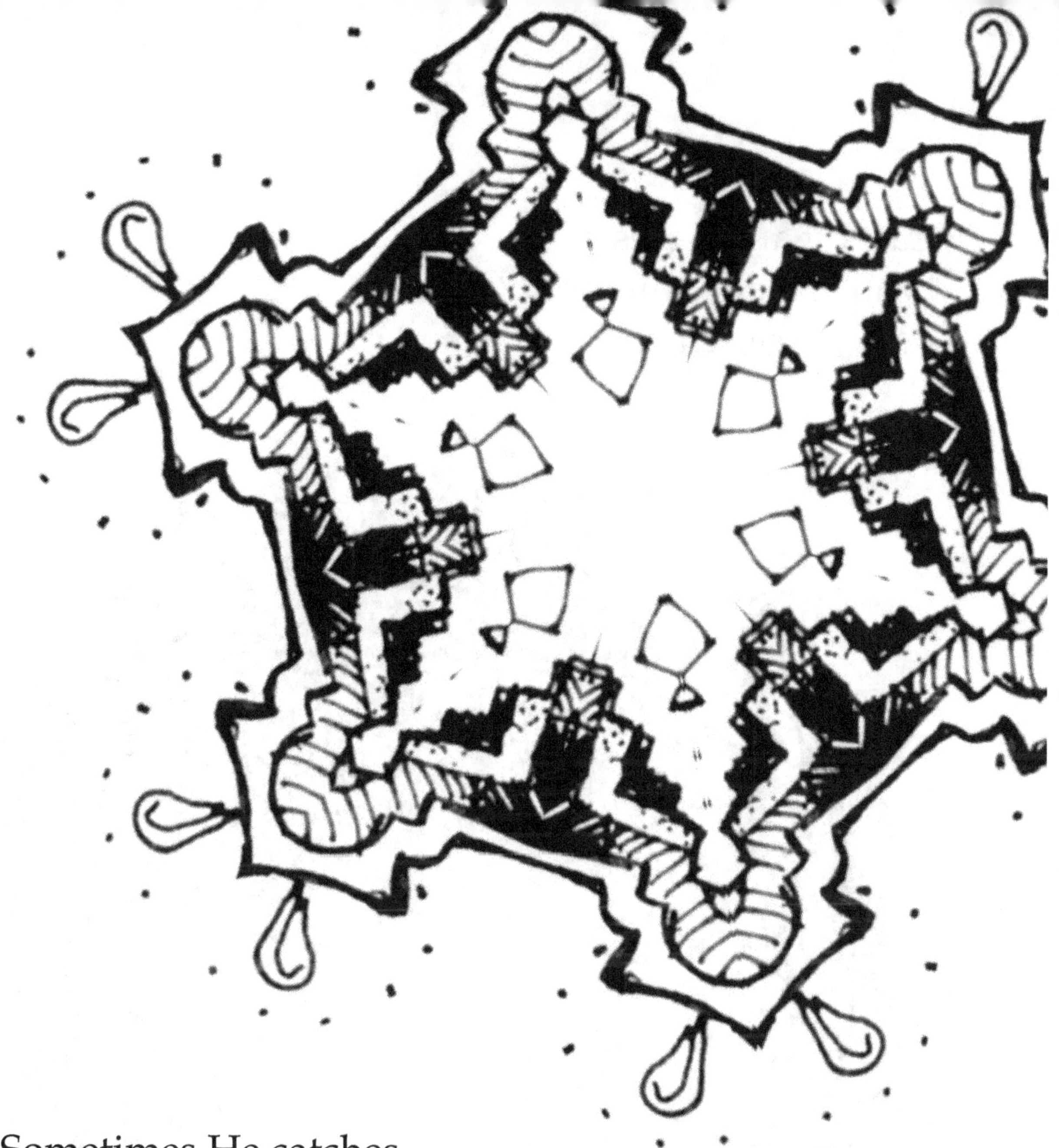

Sometimes He catches
me even before I know
I've jumped off the edge.

Cast off all images.
Who you *are*, you cannot see.
Being, not seeing.

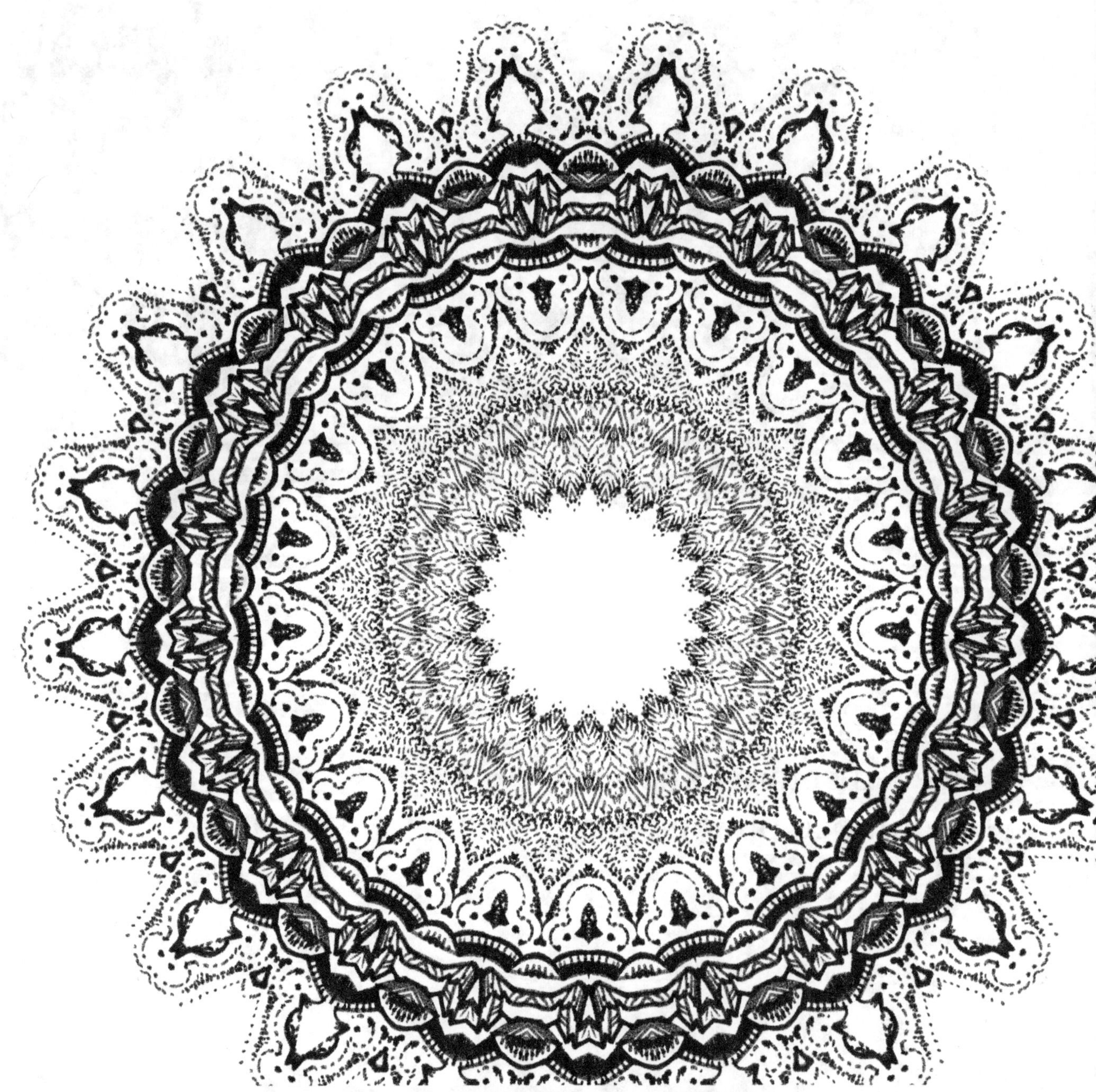

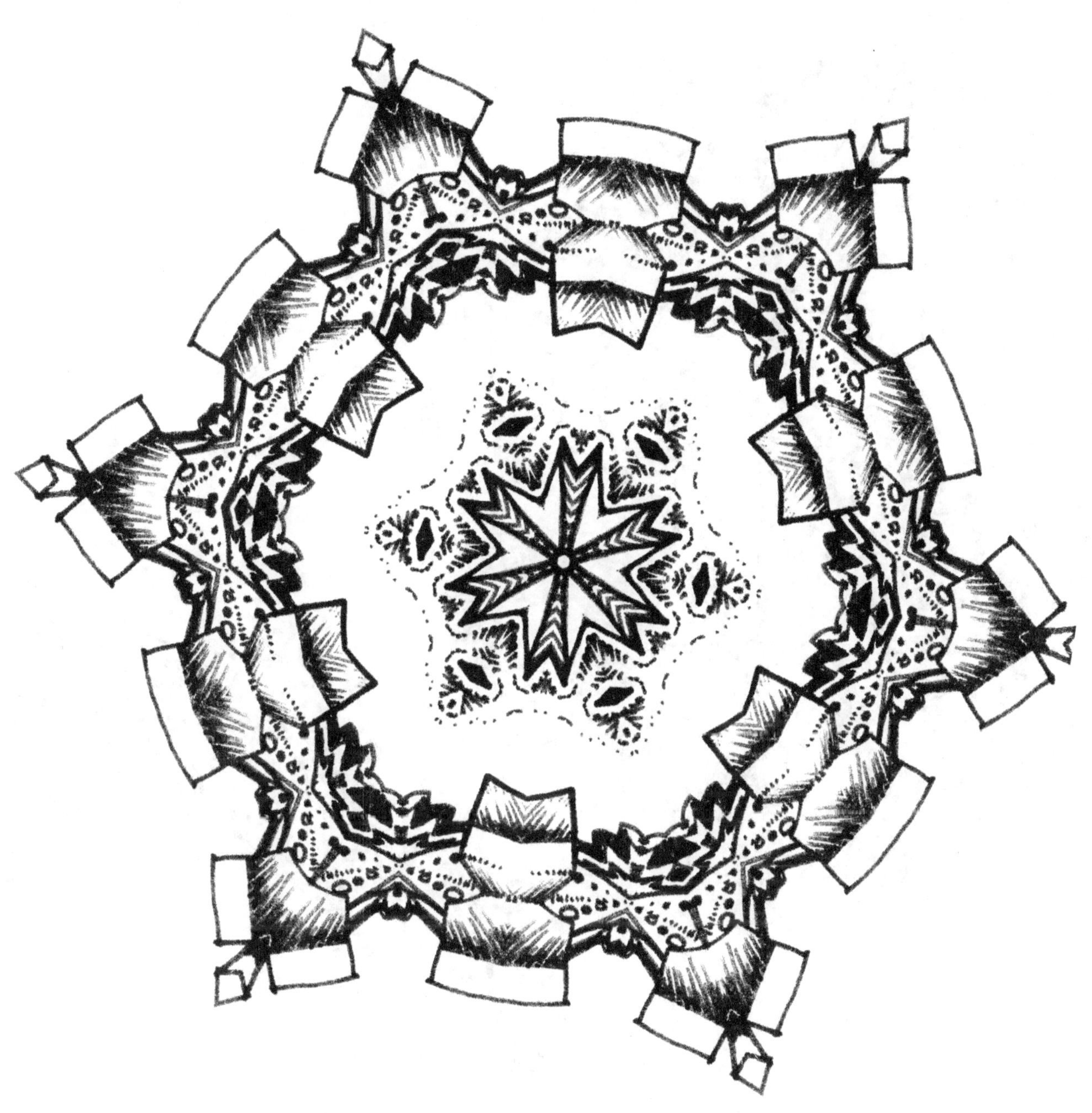

This body-mind-heart
represents its version of God.
Silence in its eyes.

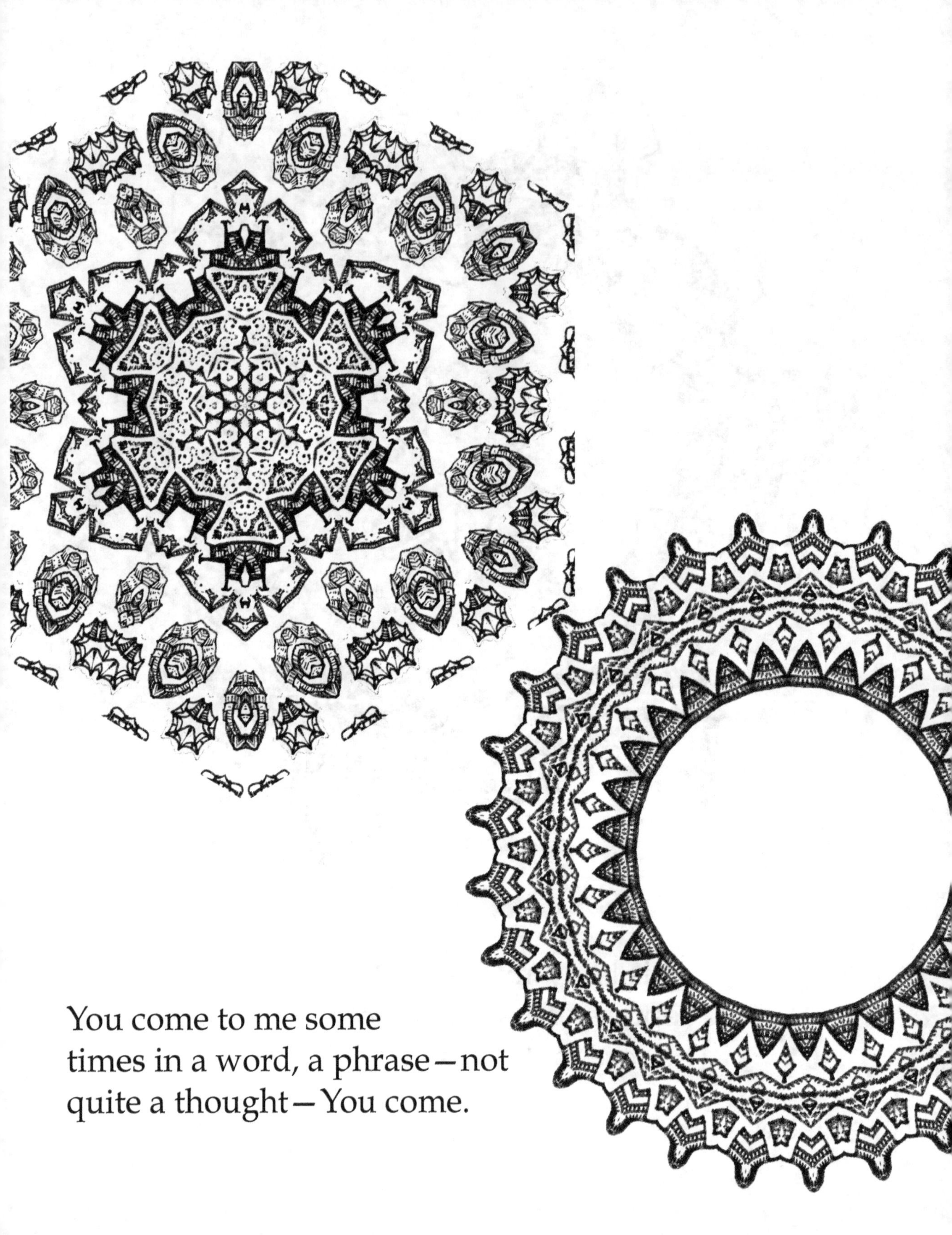

You come to me some
times in a word, a phrase—not
quite a thought—You come.

He wants to keep me
coming, so He takes me slow,
and keeps me coming.

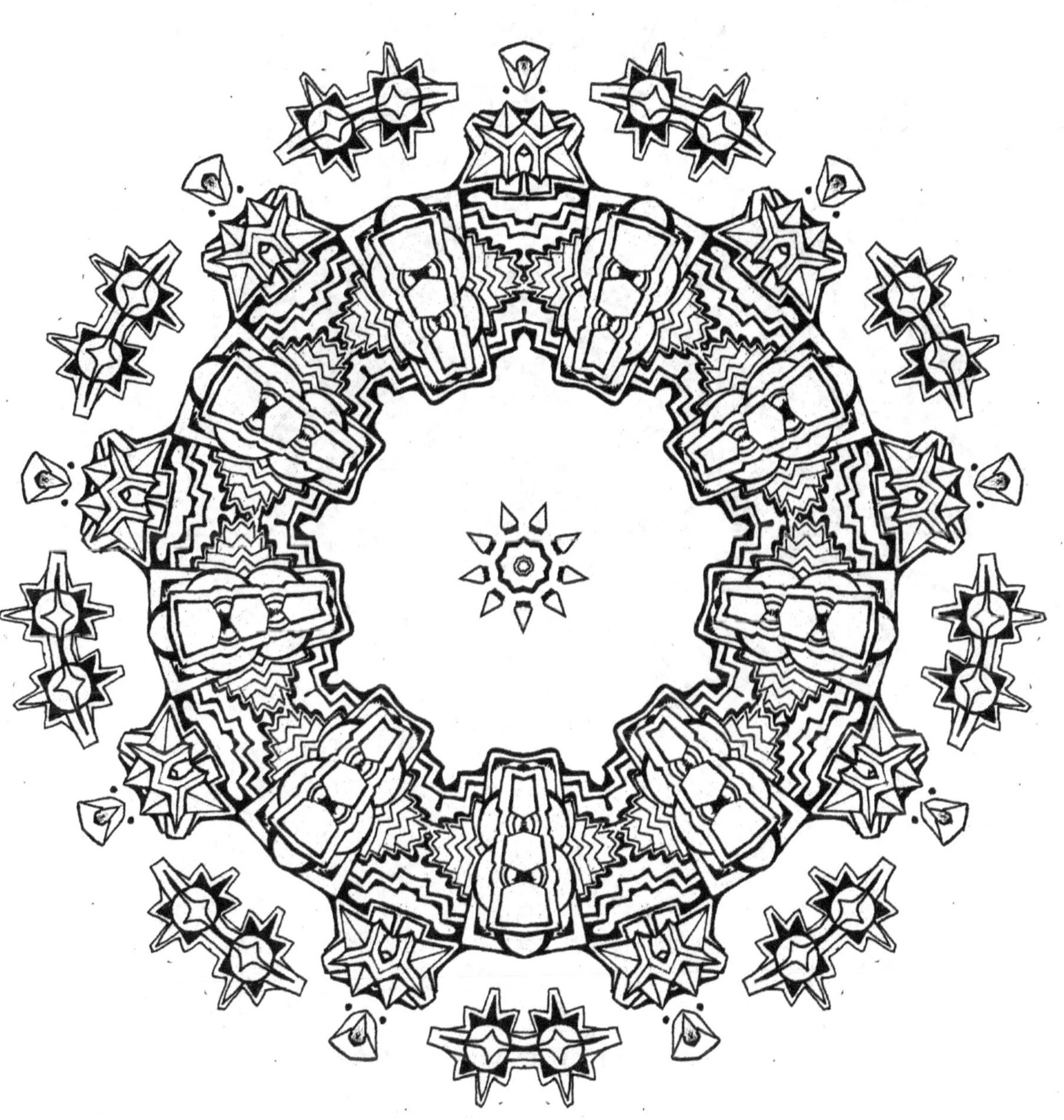

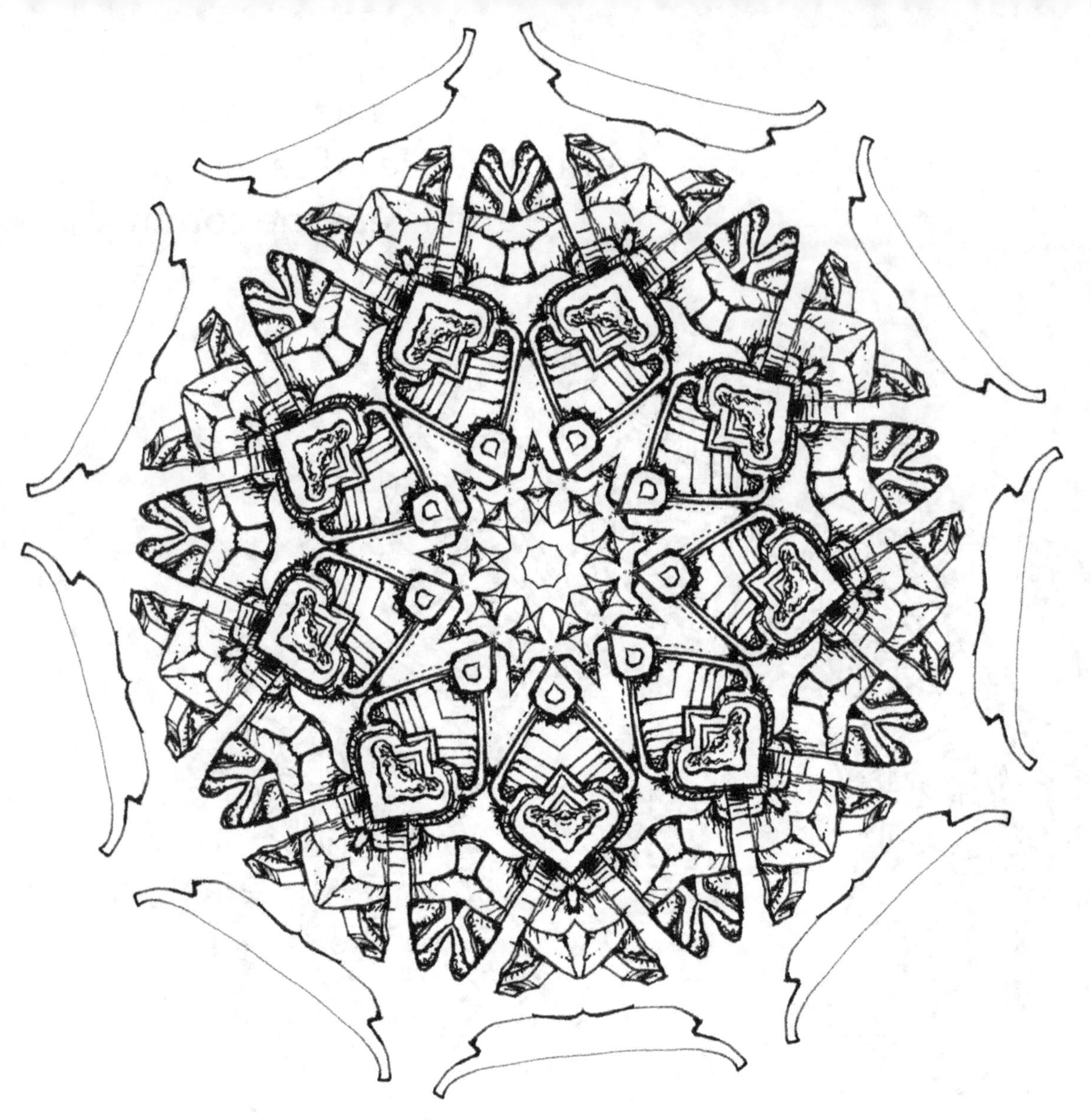

Finally, Baba's
Love wave washes over us—
we swirl with delight.

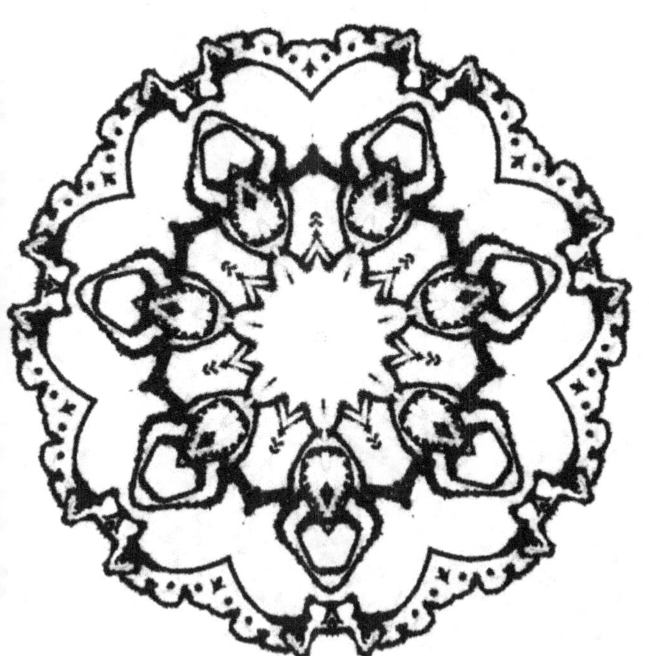

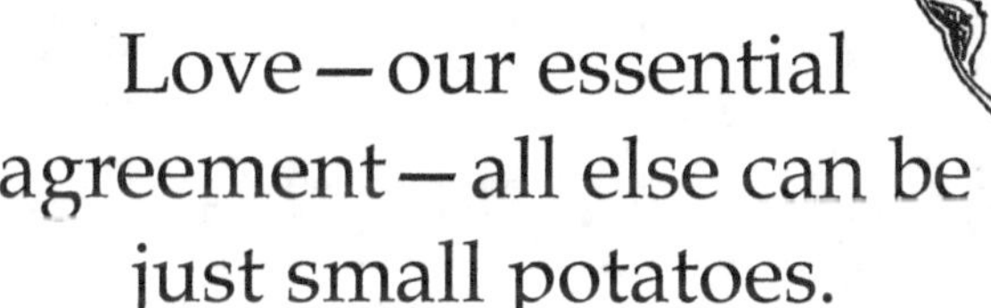

Love — our essential
agreement — all else can be
just small potatoes.

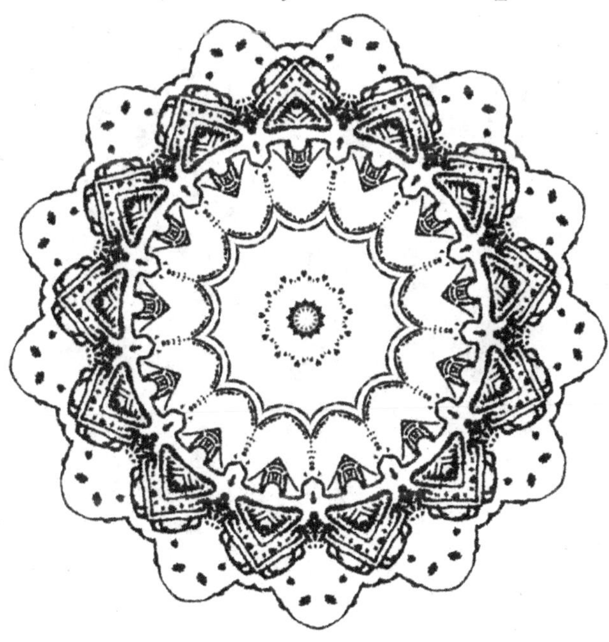

Memory faded,
yet Love never forgotten,
Your Name remains, Lord.

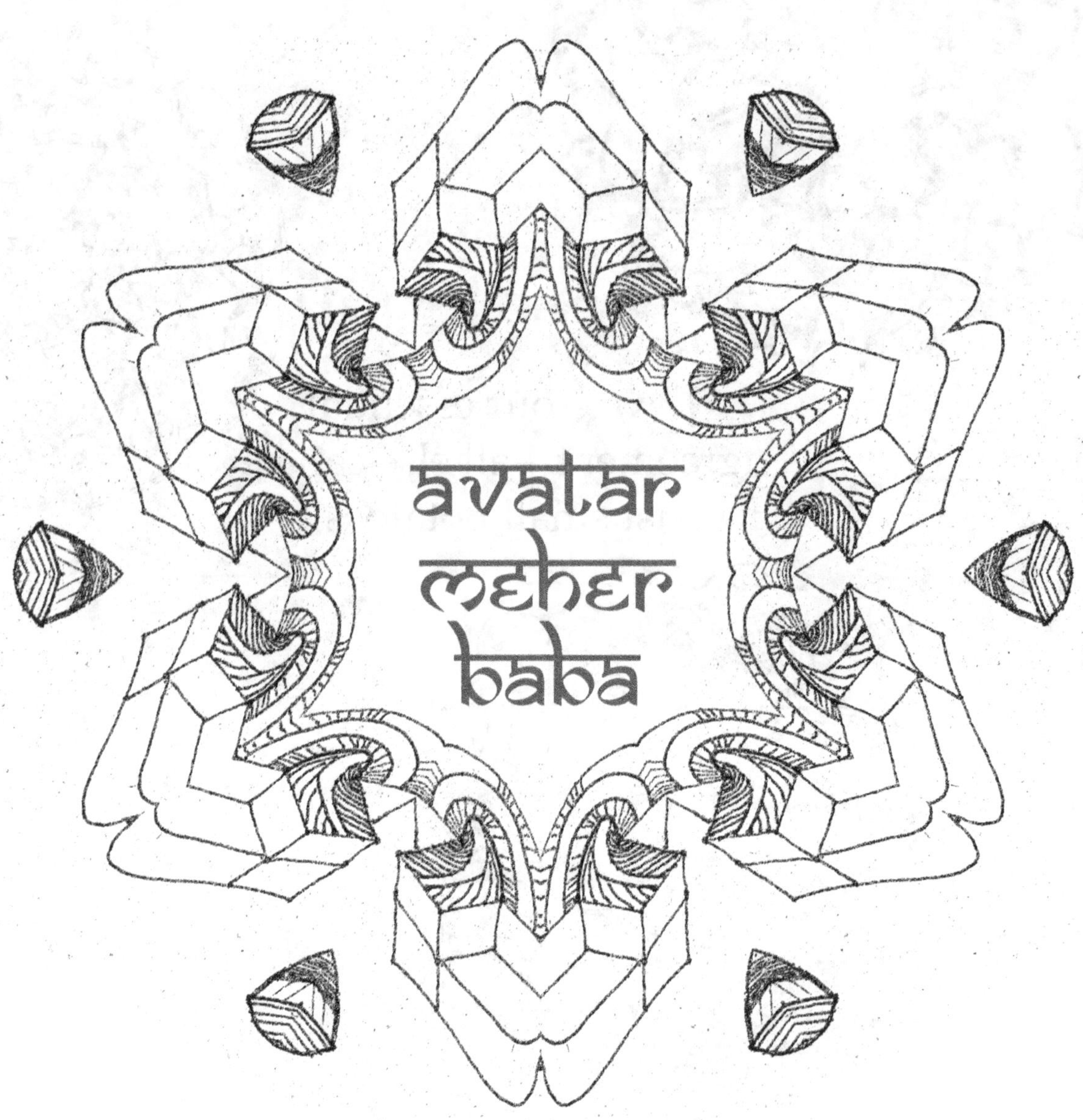

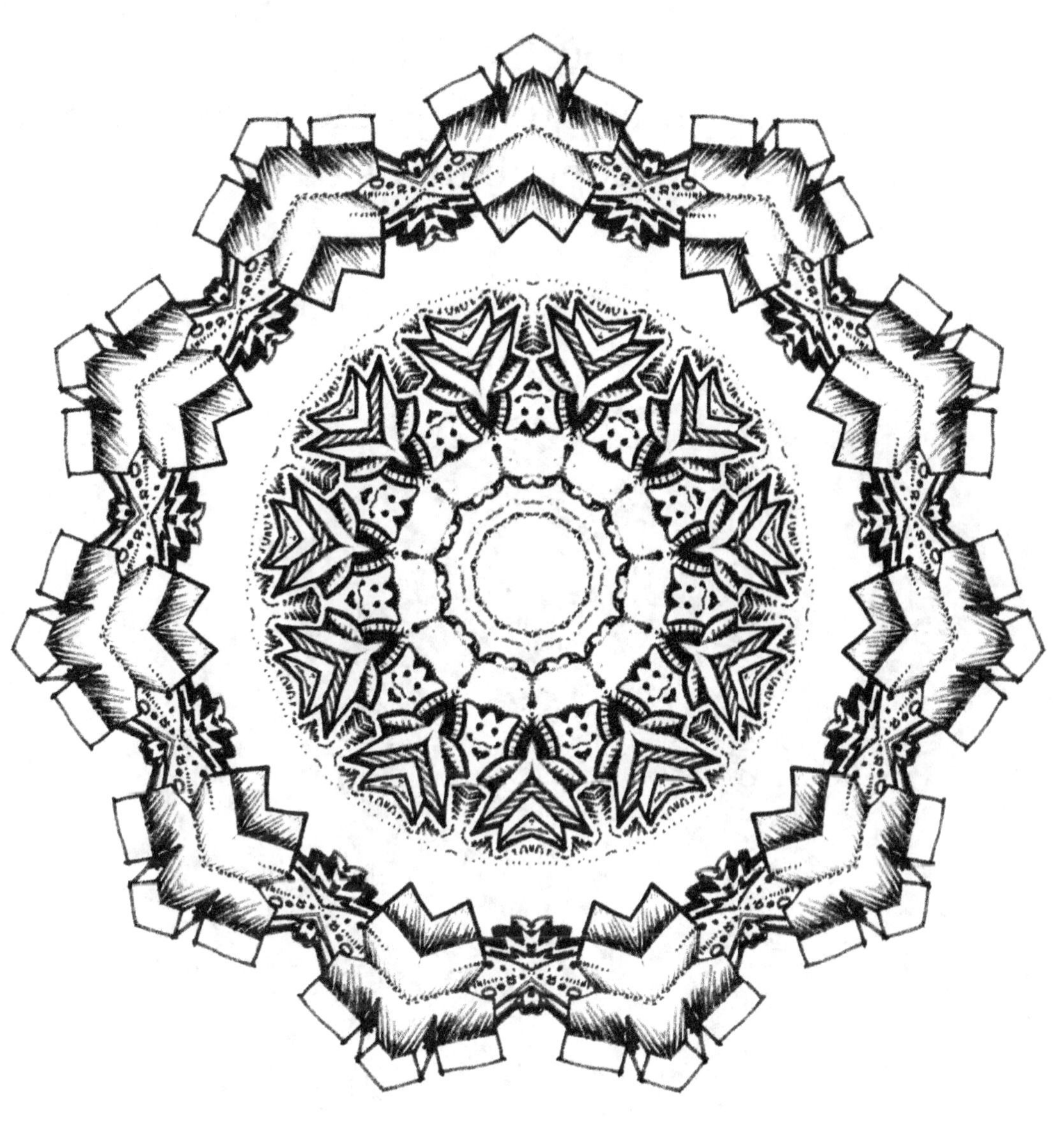

I sit still. Quiet
my mind, keep Your Divine face
within my closed eyes.

By Your Love I am
drawn through the maze of karma.
I accept all that's passed.

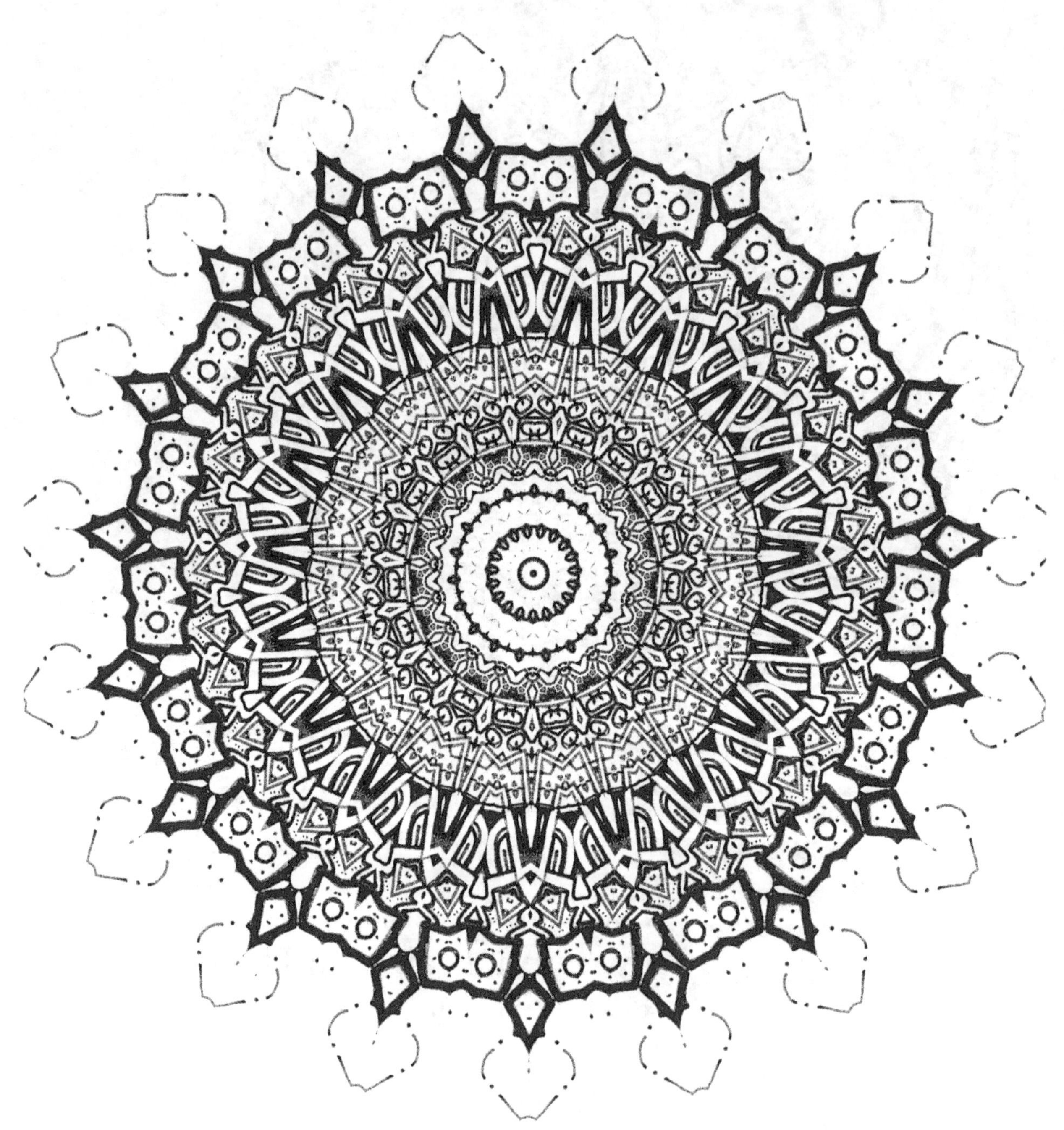

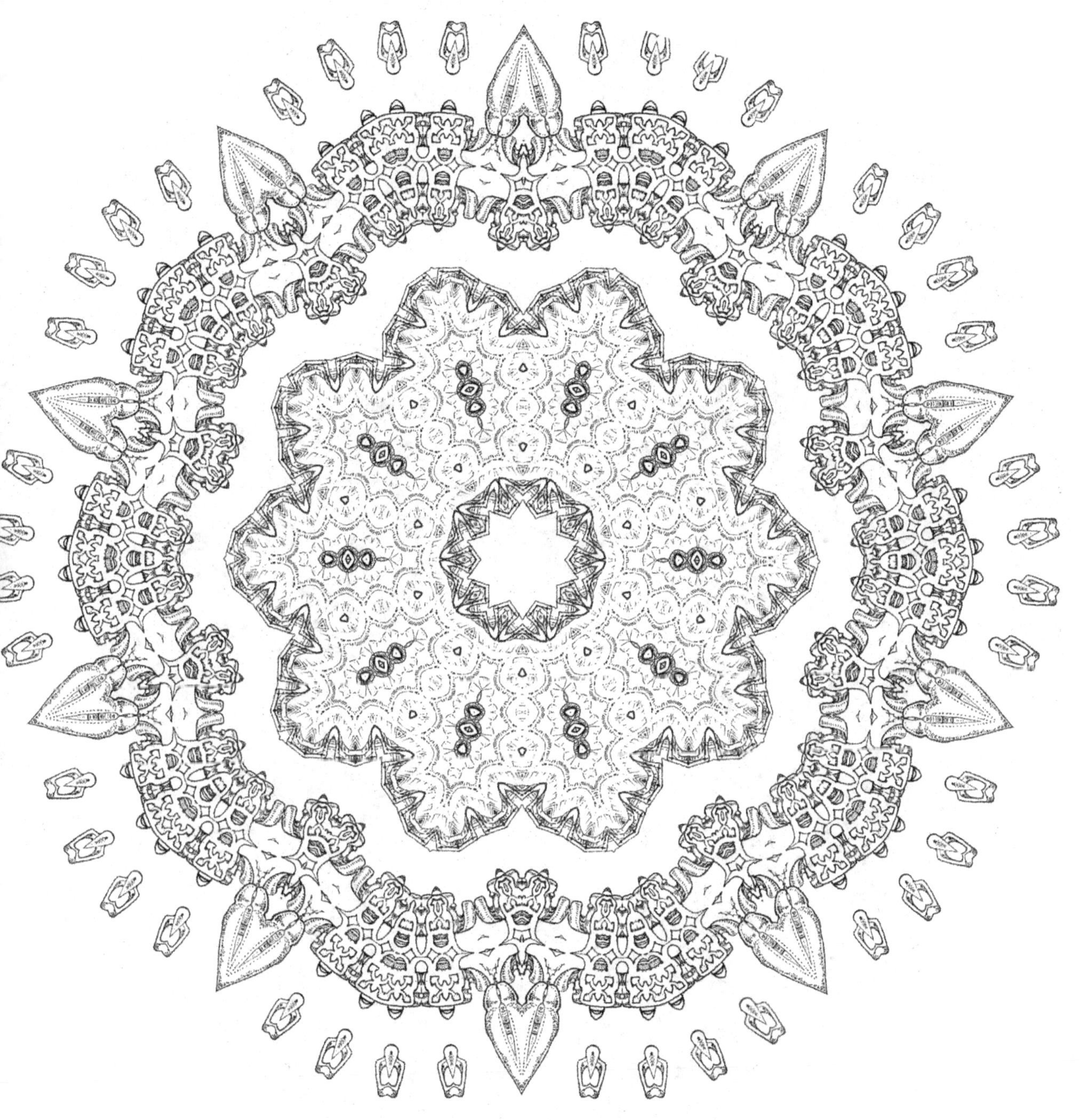

In this paradox
allow the mystery to be…
no solving of Love.

May Your precious Love
shine in my heart, through my eyes
and, please, through my voice.

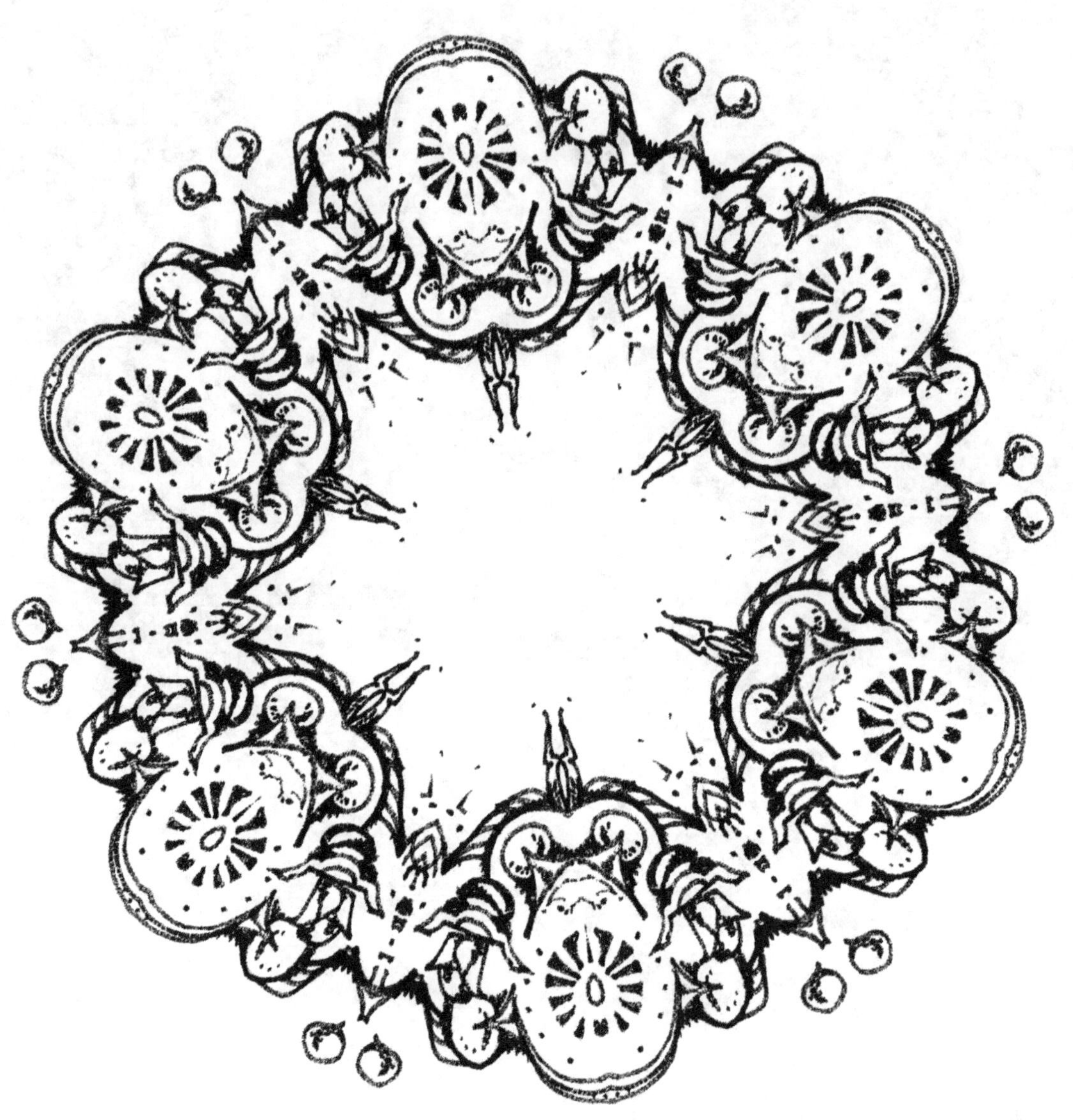

Mehera

placed as a last kiss–
her very fine handkerchief
on Her Beloved's face.

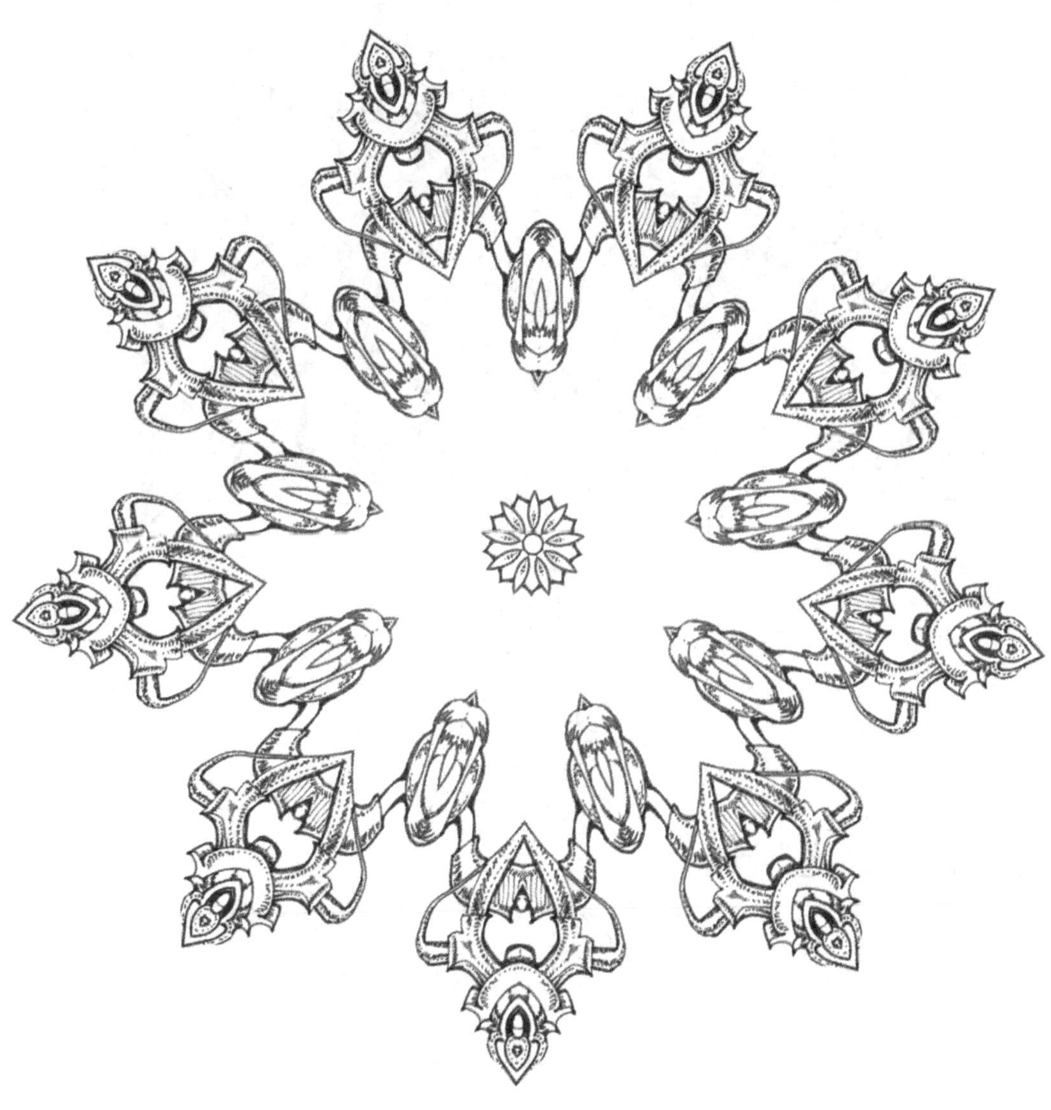

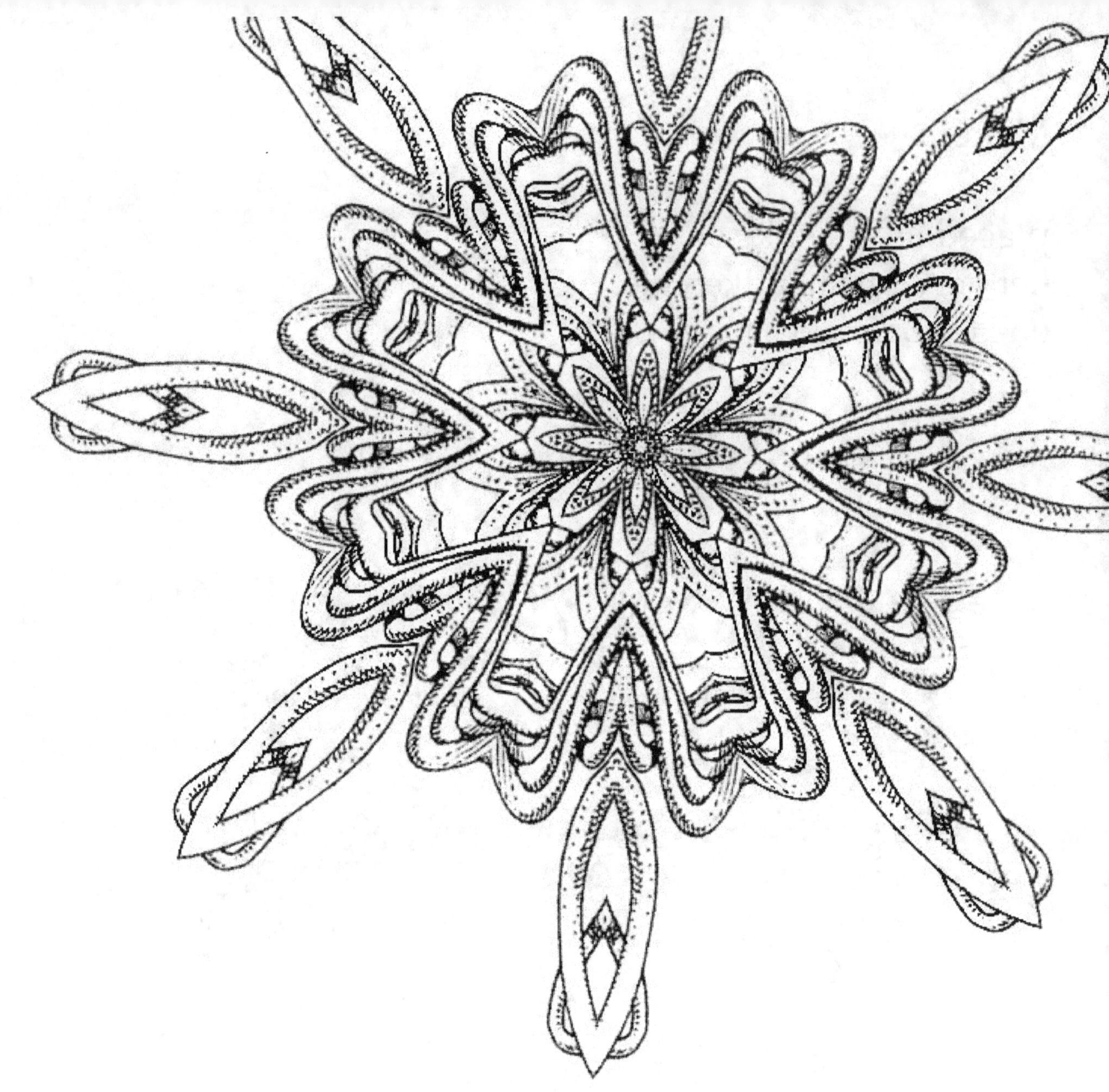

Is it time? Will You
come? Is it time? Can I go?
Will I come to You?

Right-wrong no use now —
just one path to Rumi's field
mind gone — *all from heart.*

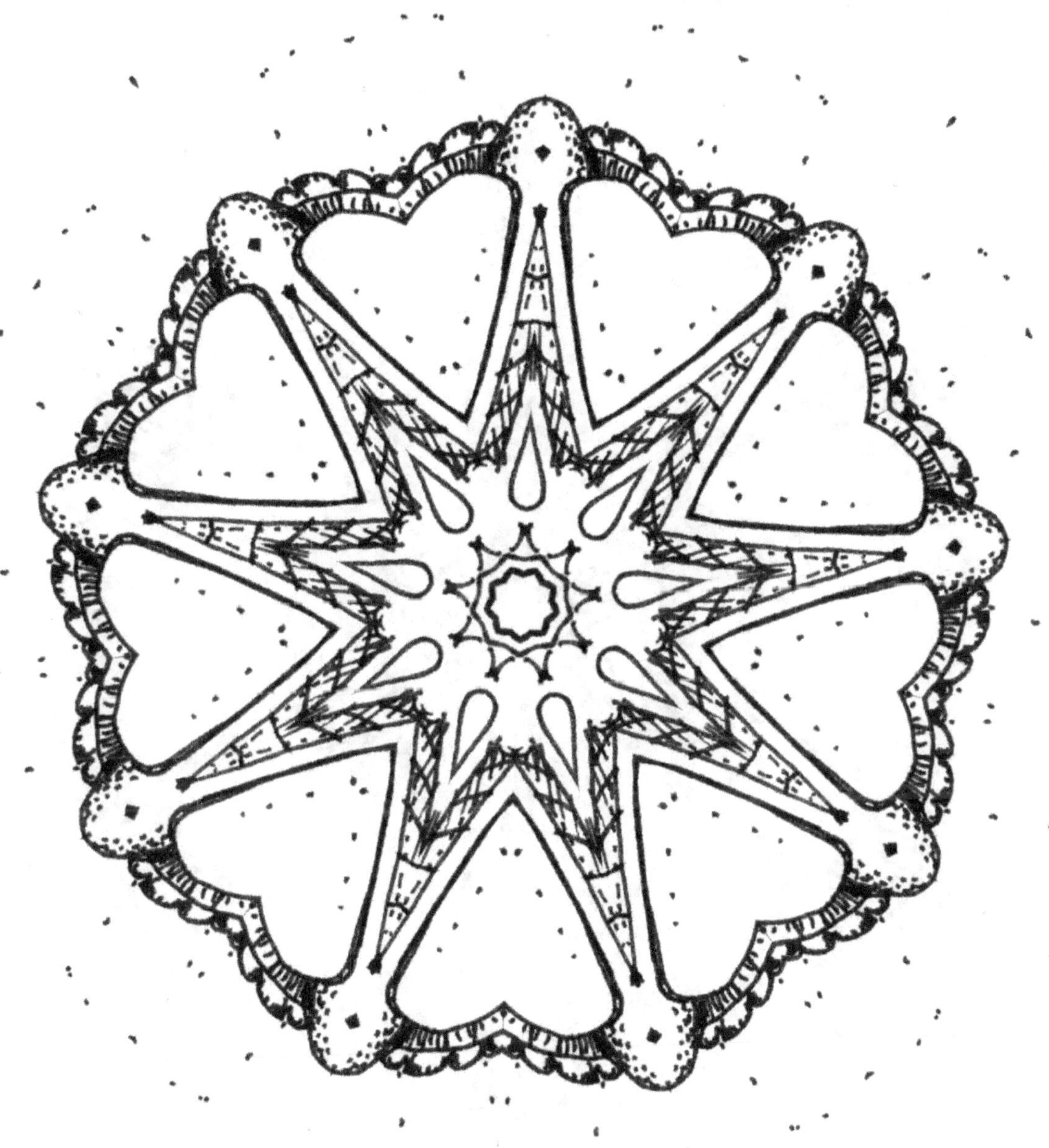

No way to keep You
but in heart's secret silence —
the path opens here.

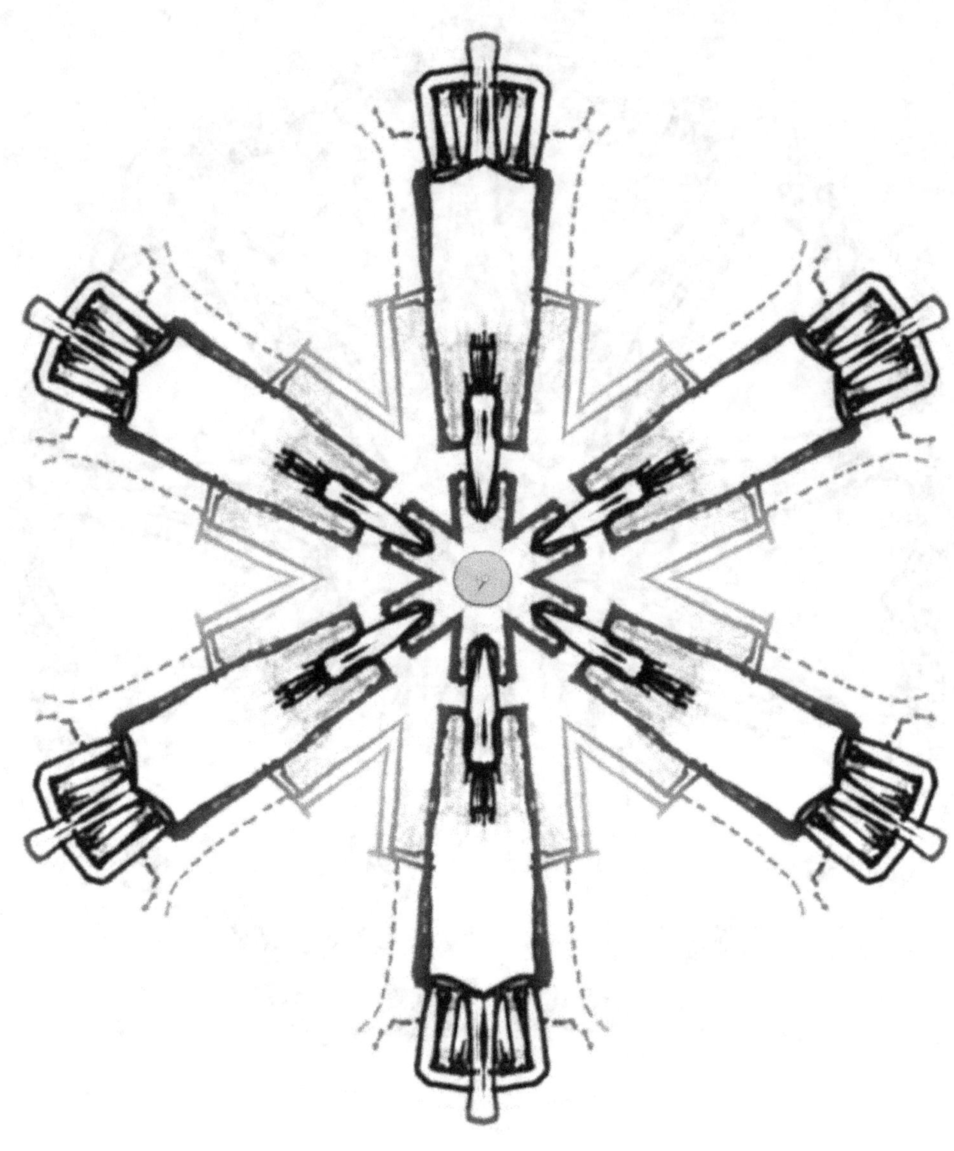

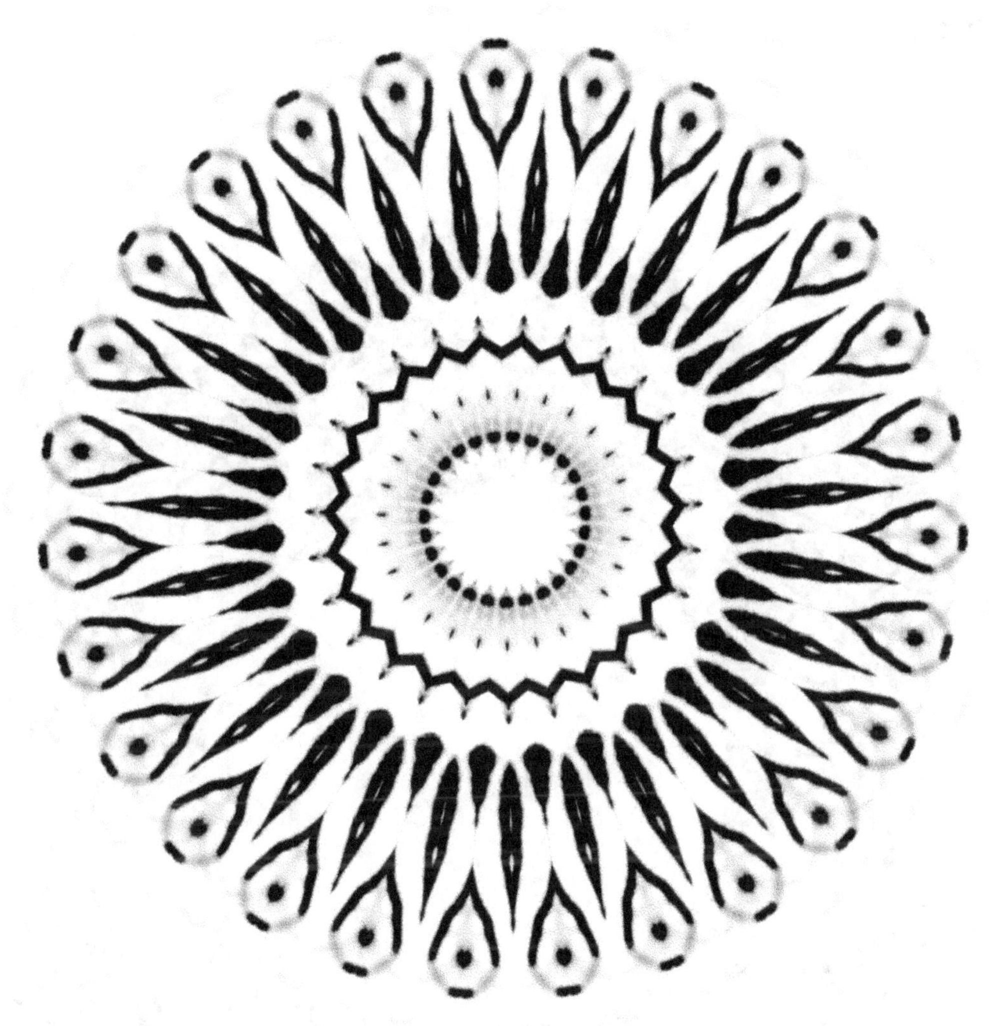

I cannot see You
sitting in the Lagoon chair —
You're not what eyes can see.

Tree trunk blown hollow—
moss edges its furrowed shell—
rooted in stillness.

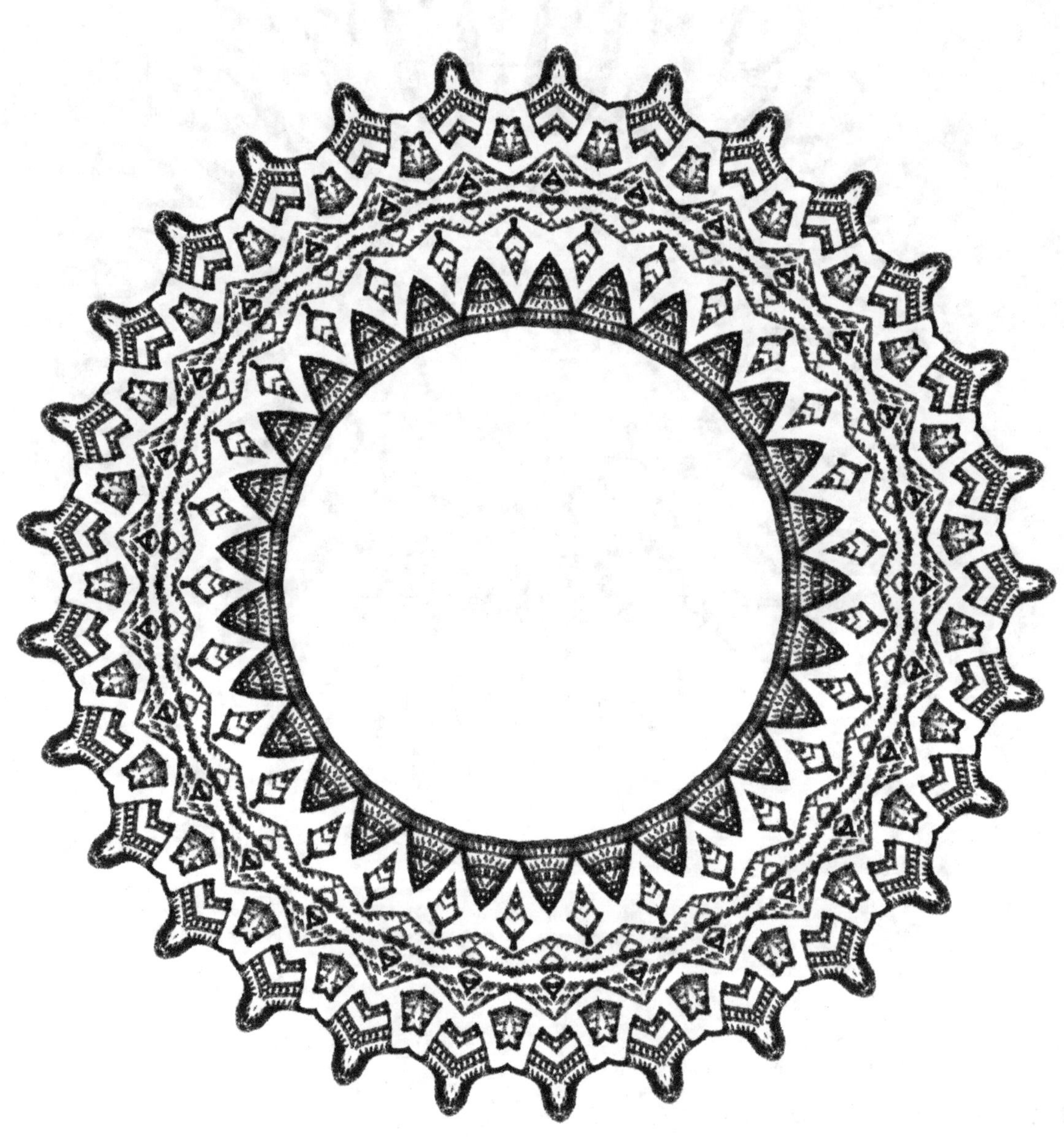

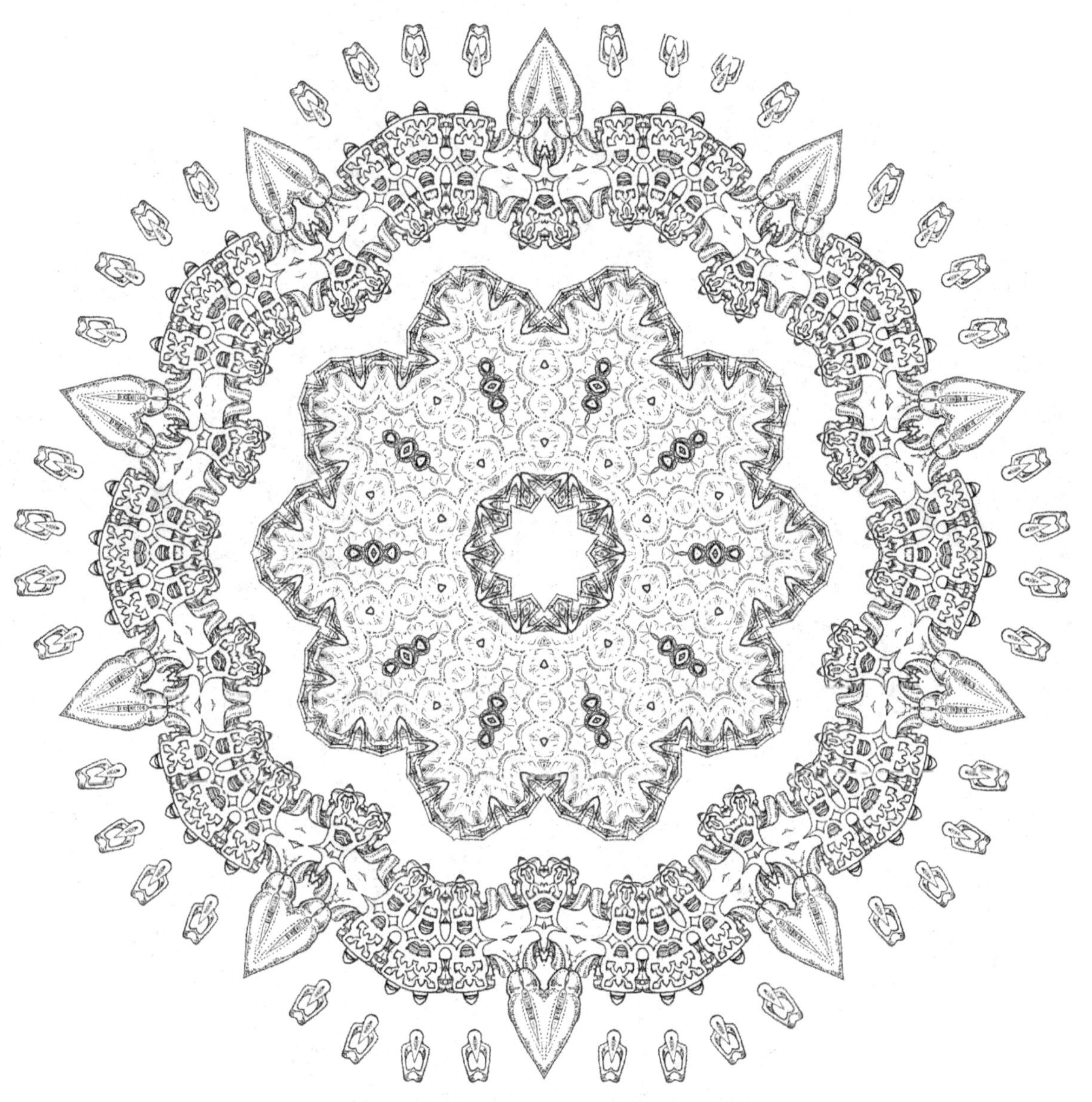

In my heart's silence
I'm supposed to talk with You —
stillness sings of love.

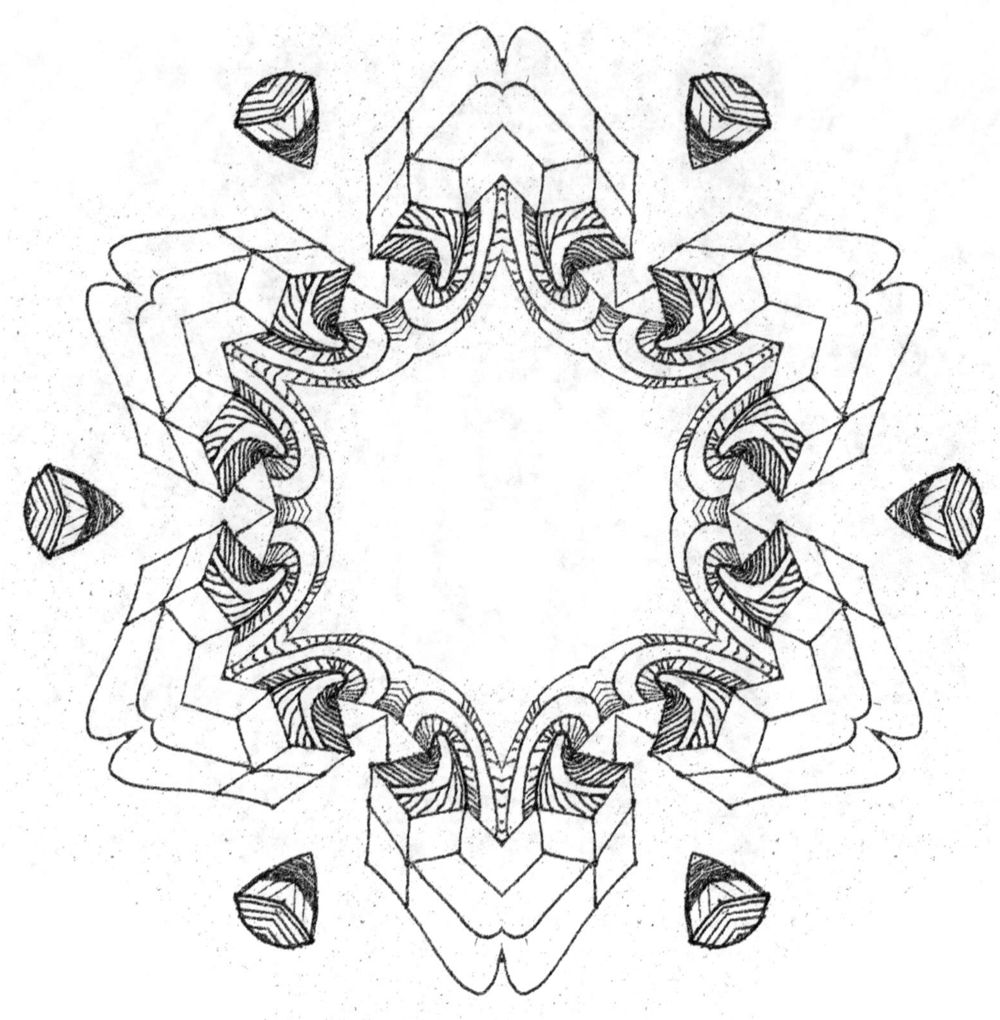

Emptiness reigns in
the autumn of this life now.
What fullness can come?

Love He gives and gives—
what is there yet to ask for?
More, more, still yet more.

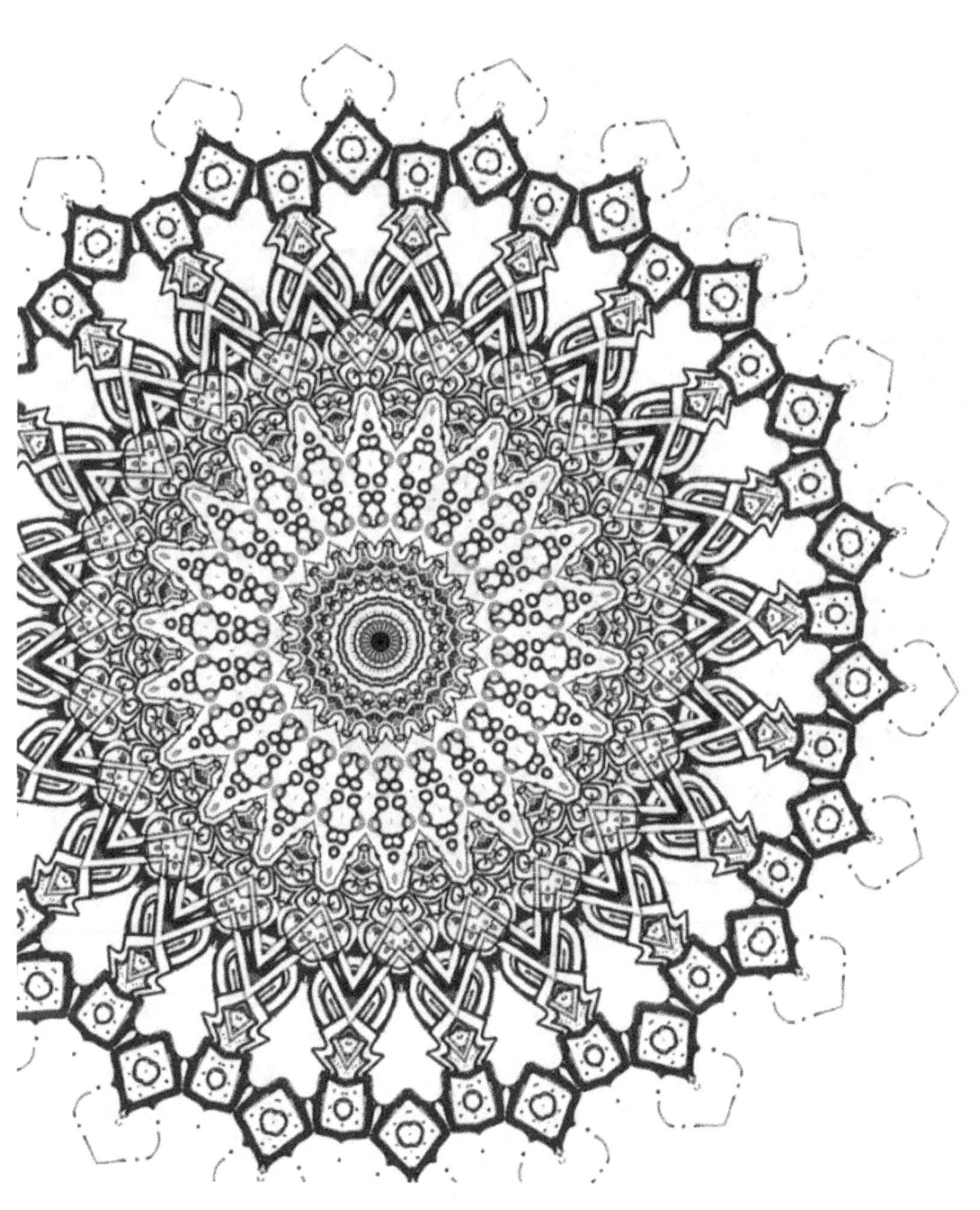

Everything I say
reminds me of other things—
silence in my heart.

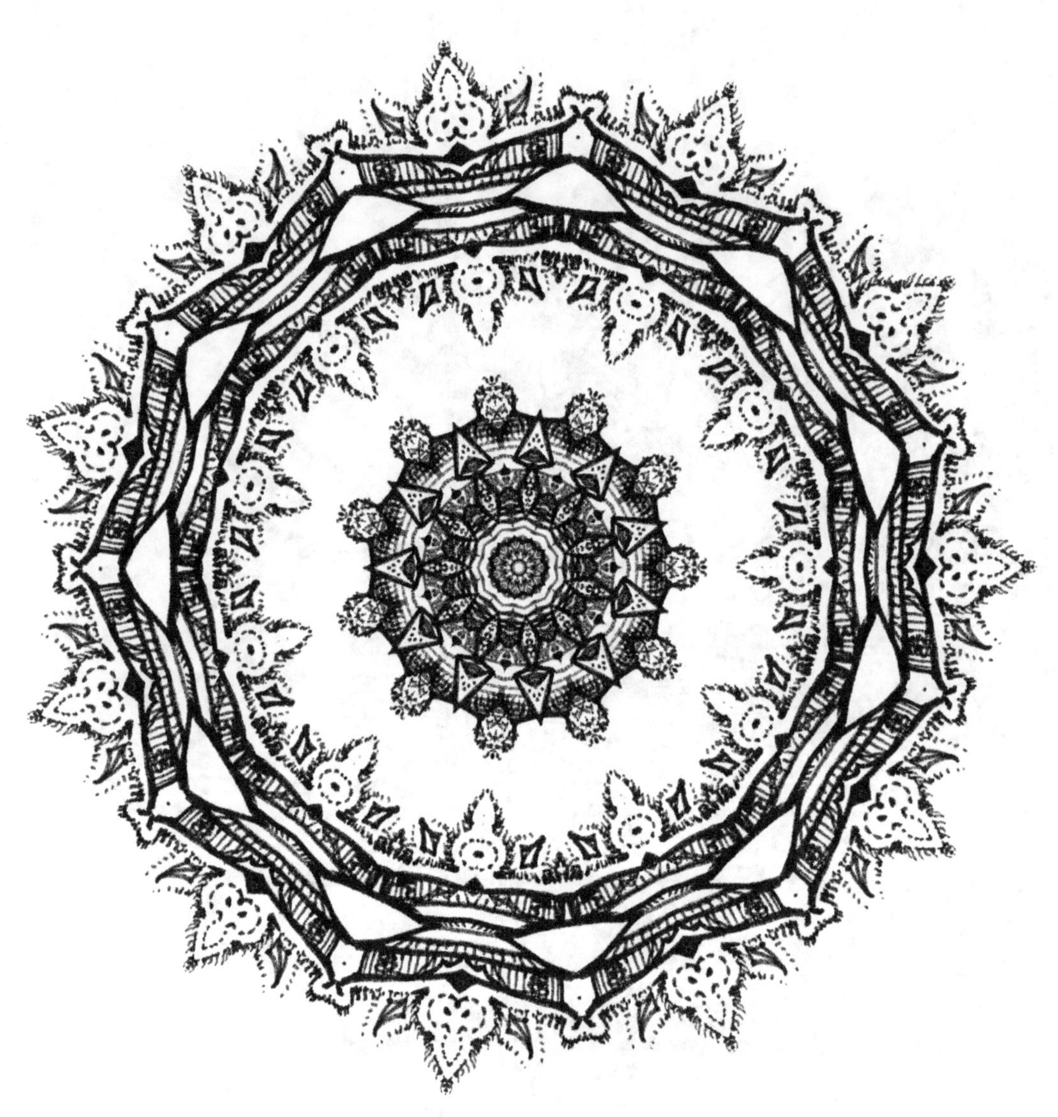

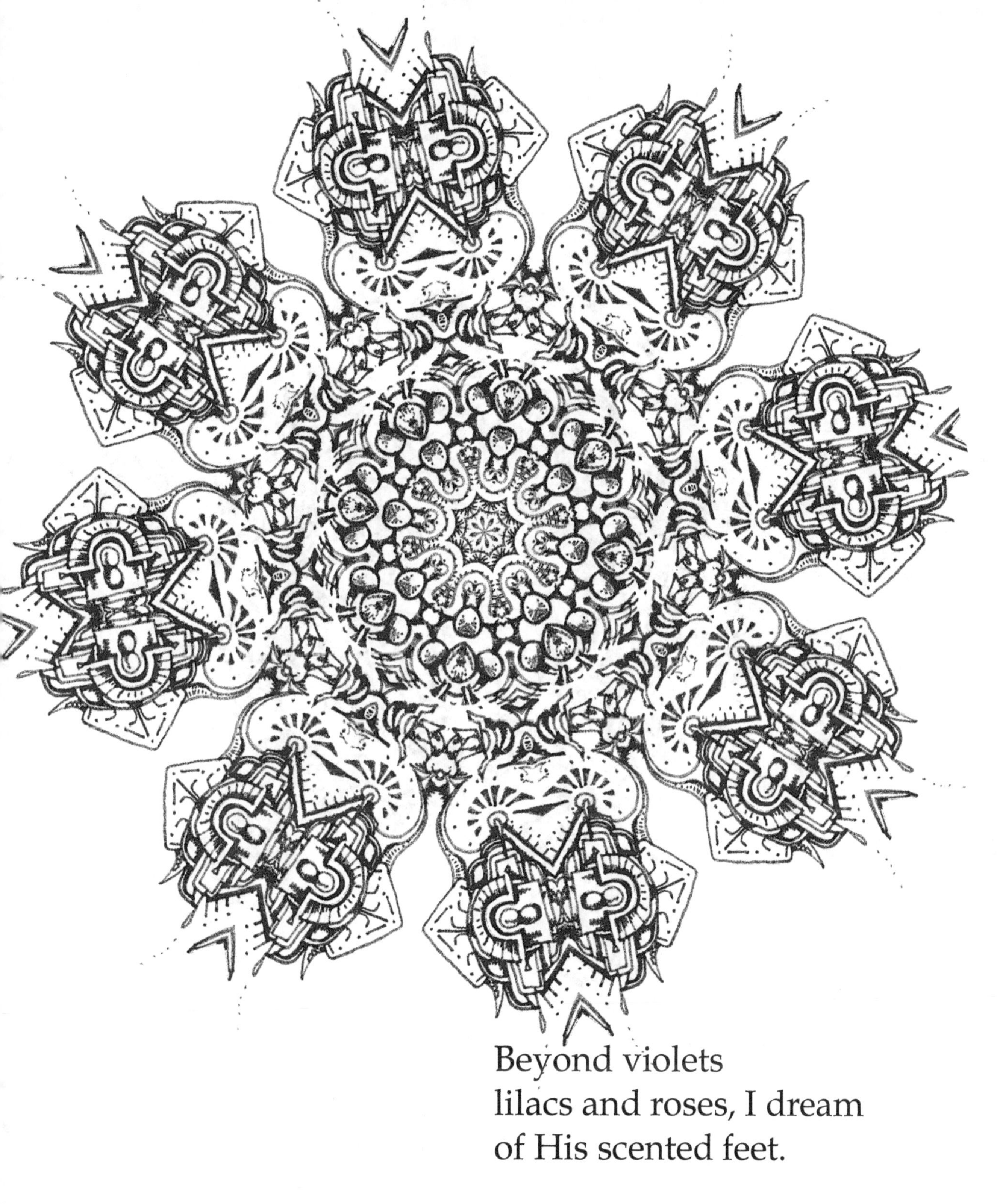

Beyond violets
lilacs and roses, I dream
of His scented feet.

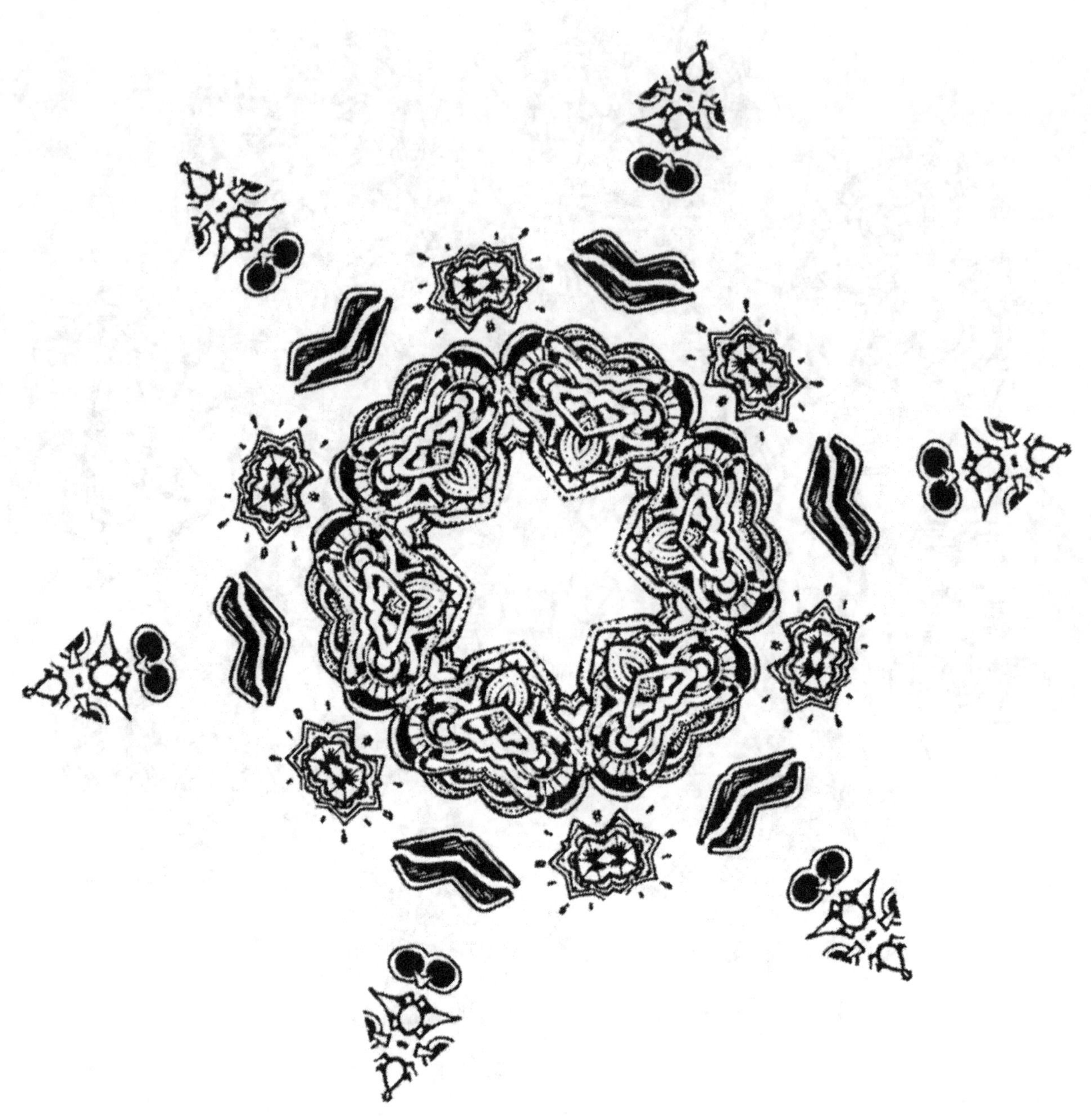

I'm forever from
somewhere else — home can only
be within. With You.

I awaken. You
gently lighten up my thoughts—
words and deeds follow.

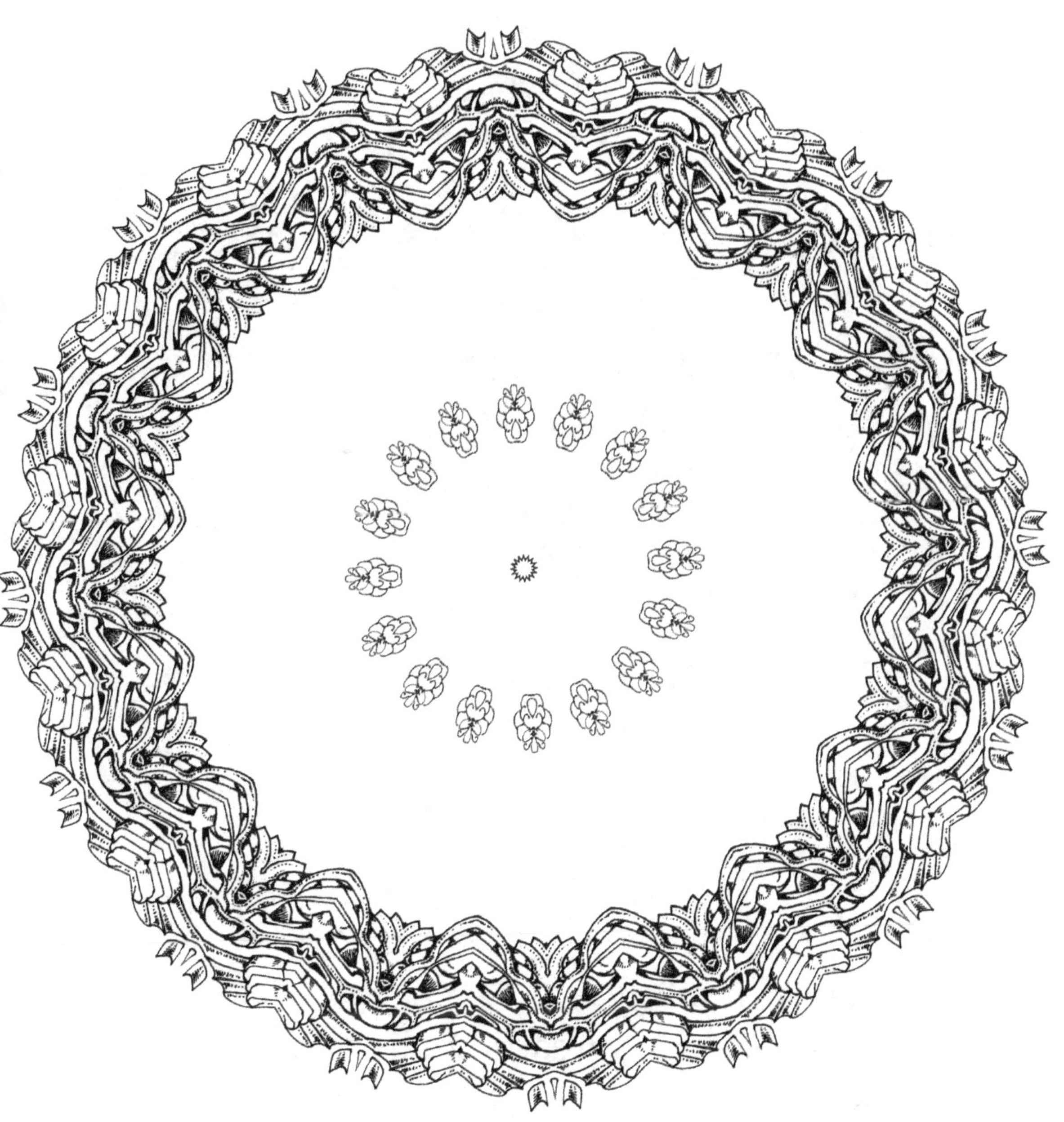

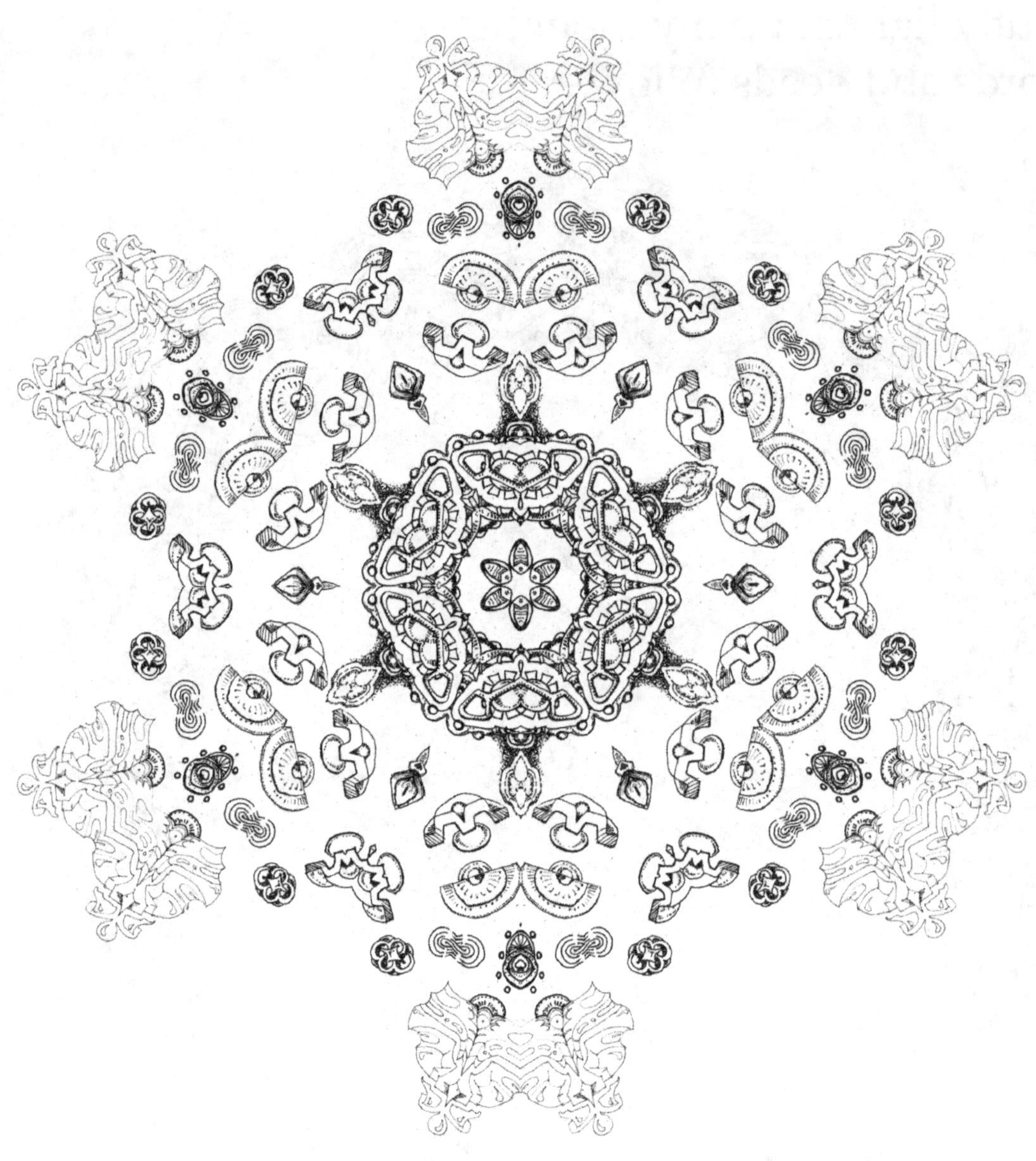

I am one of many —
Love's network spreading His name.
Golden filigrees!

How splendidly You
have managed my life so far!
How to want anything!?

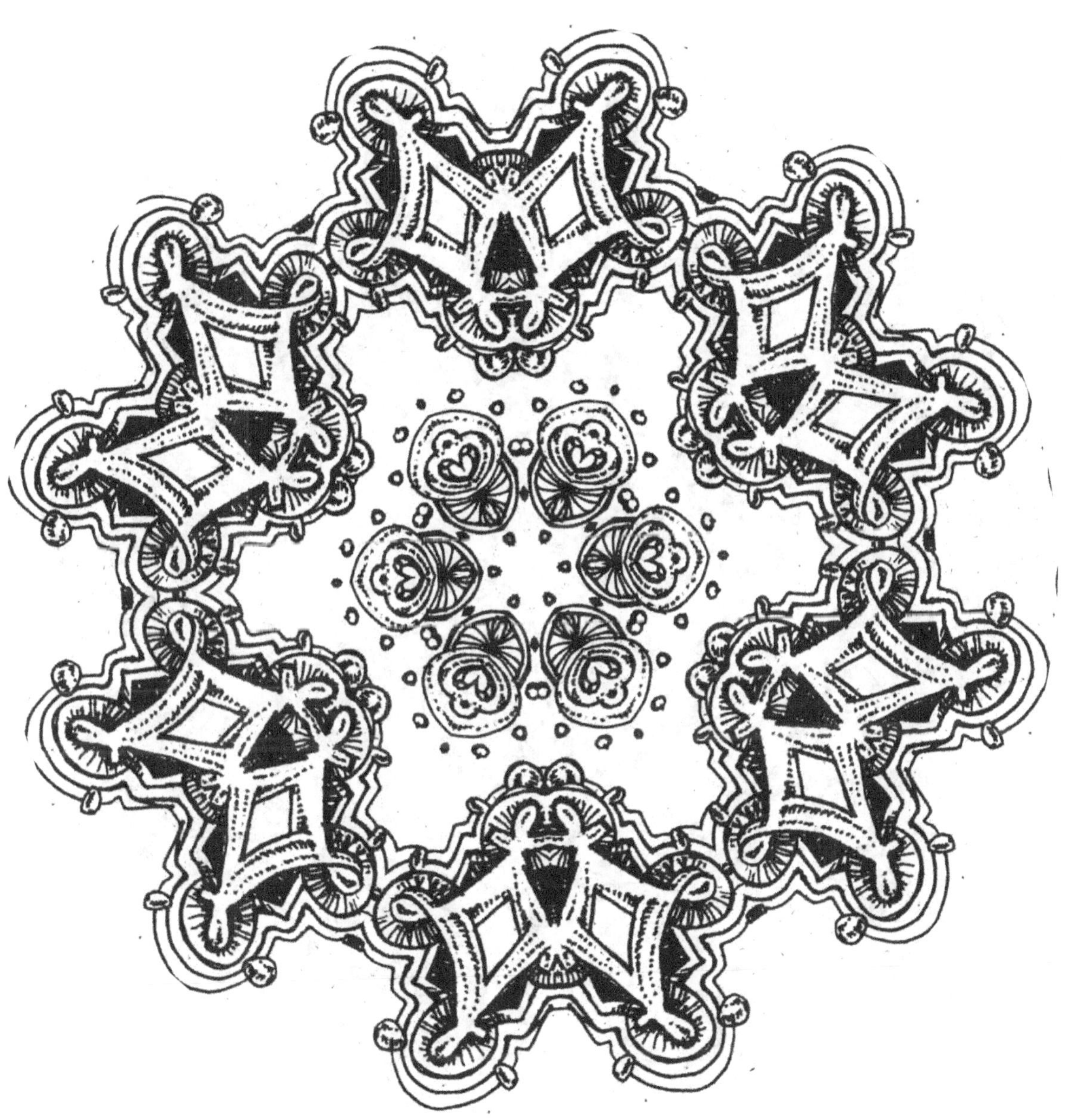

Every moment gives
opportunity—release
that gnawing desire!

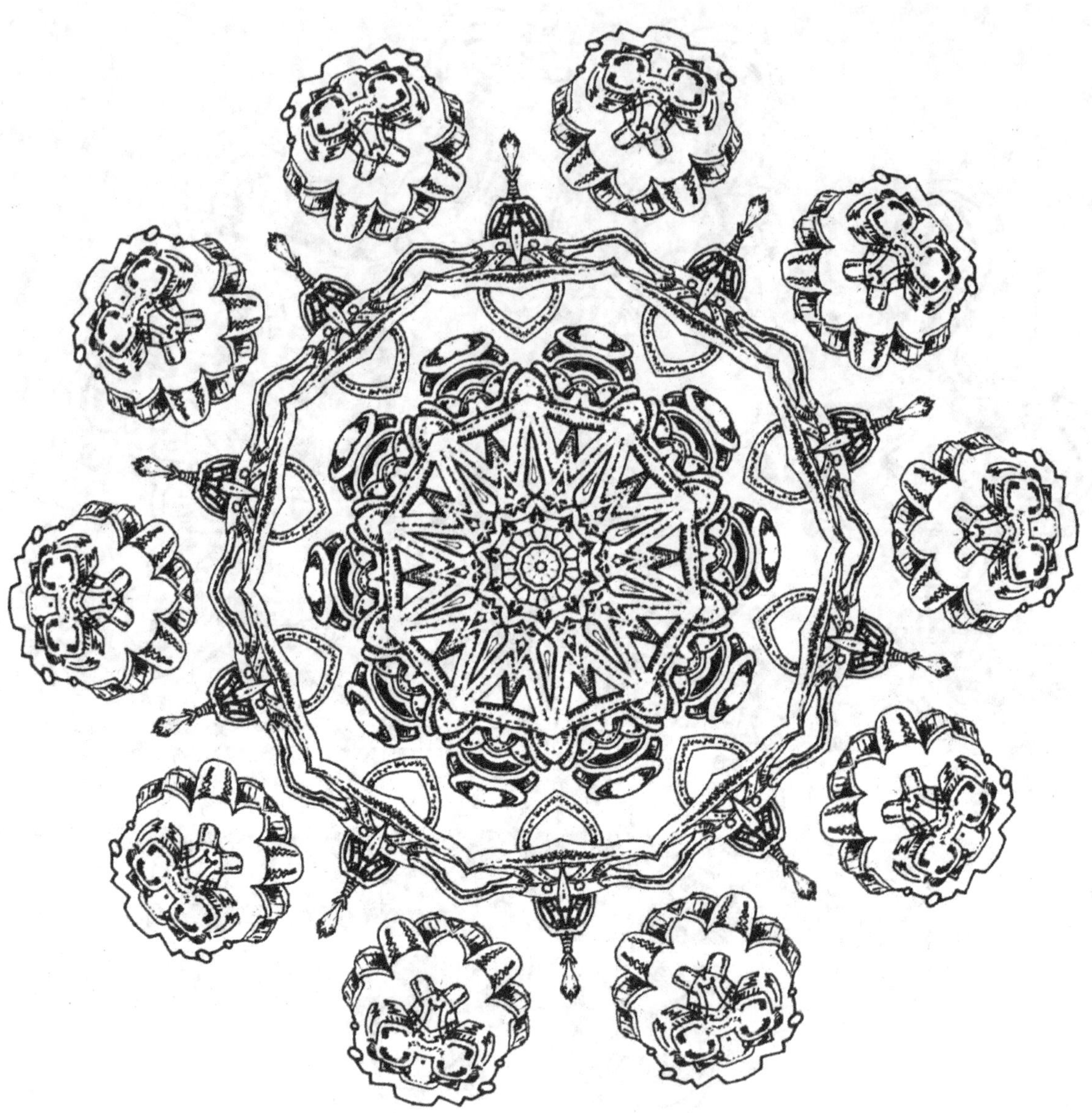

Greedy for Your gaze
upon me, upon me — for
Your gaze upon me.

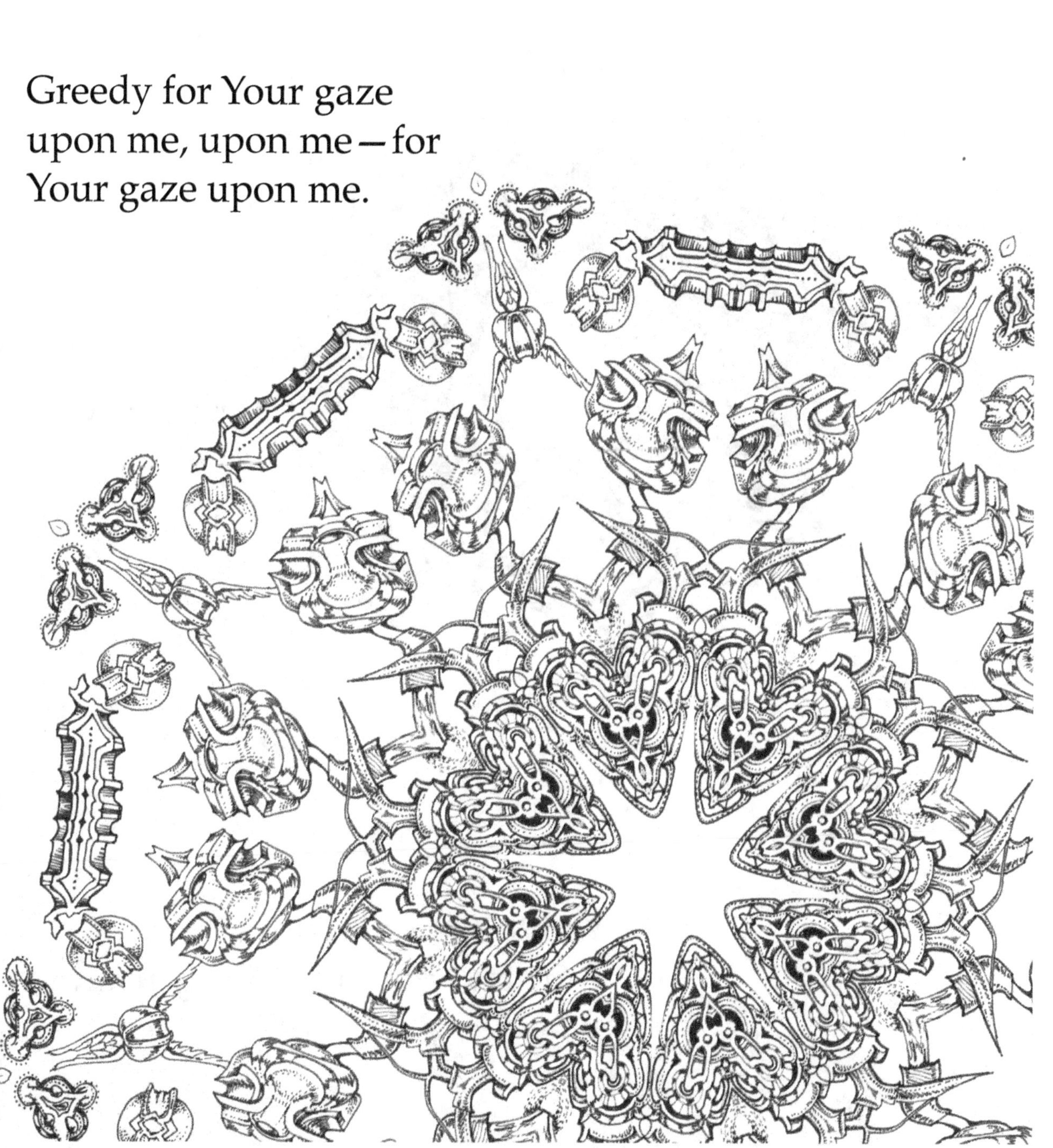

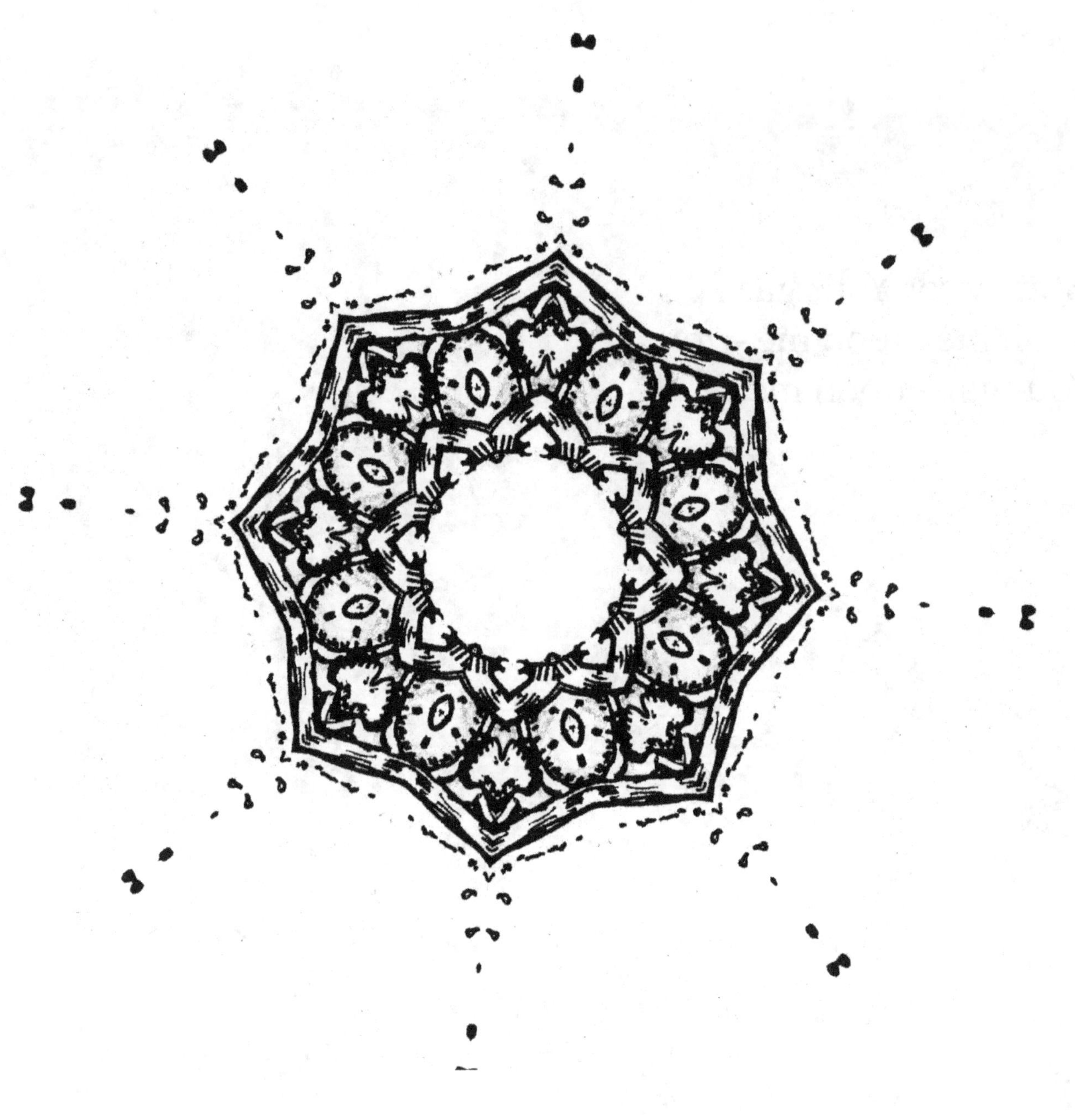

Your quiet Love stays,
and stays my mind as my heart
says, *yes, yes, oh yes!*

In our stories, we present
our moments with Him as gems.
Precious on blue velvet.

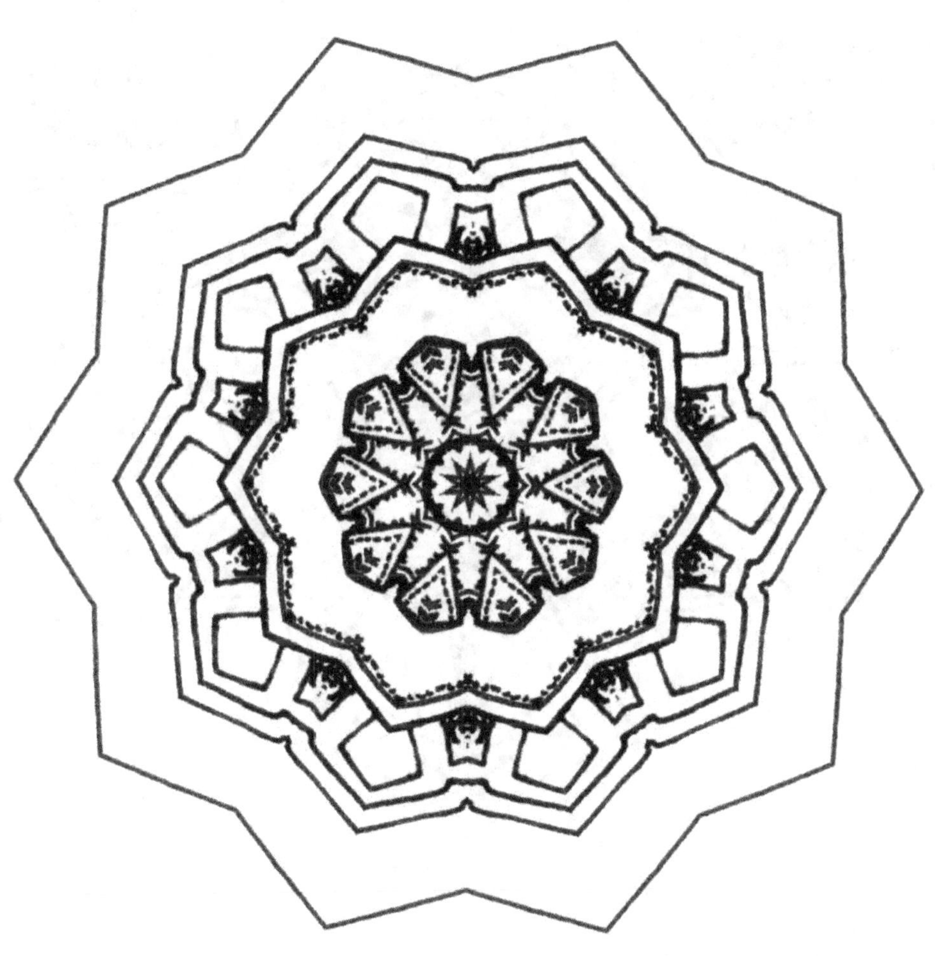

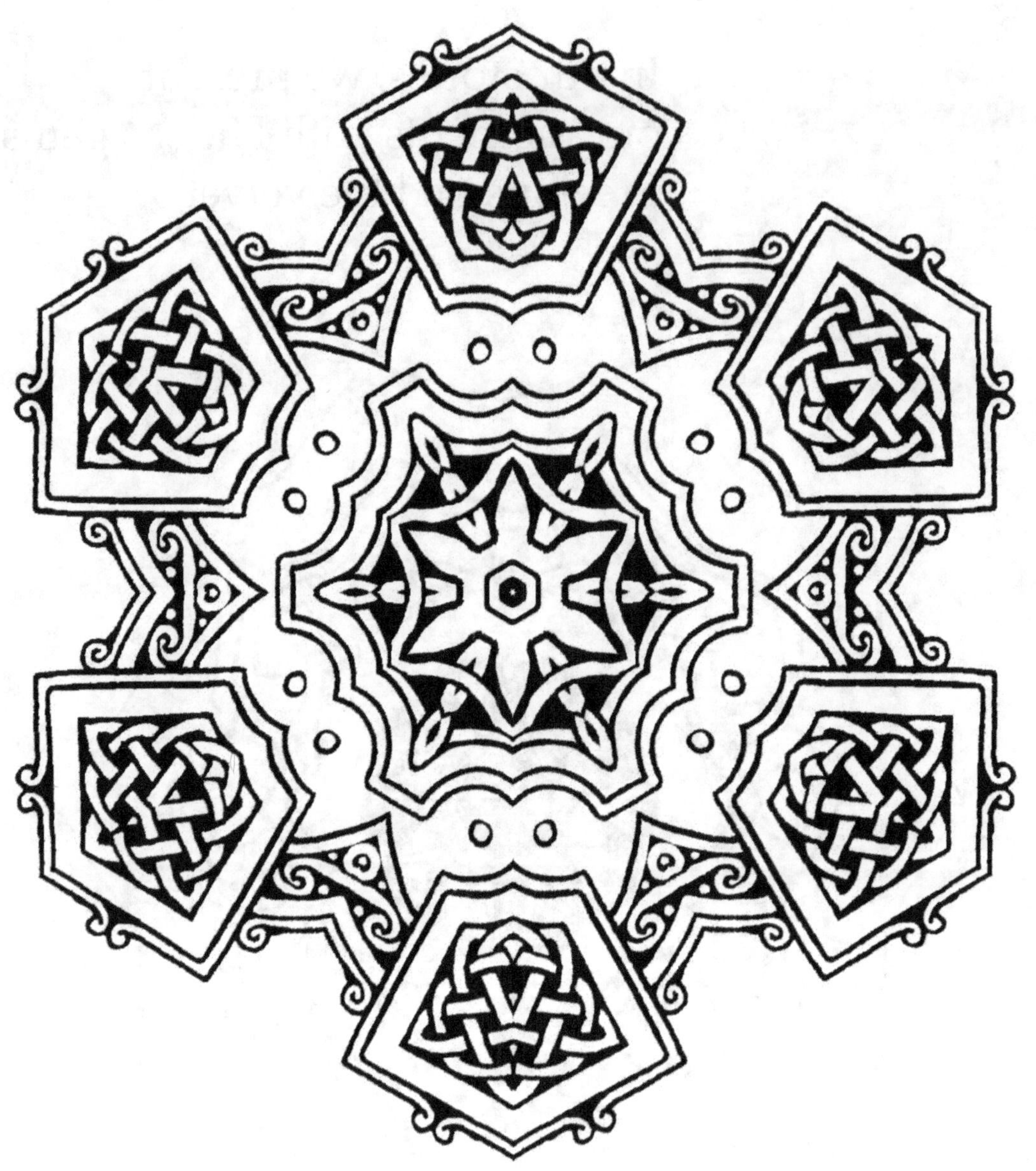

Home is when and where
I am at one with my Self.
God kissing my eyes.

At Your silent shore
I come upon words like pebbles,
sea-smooth abundance.

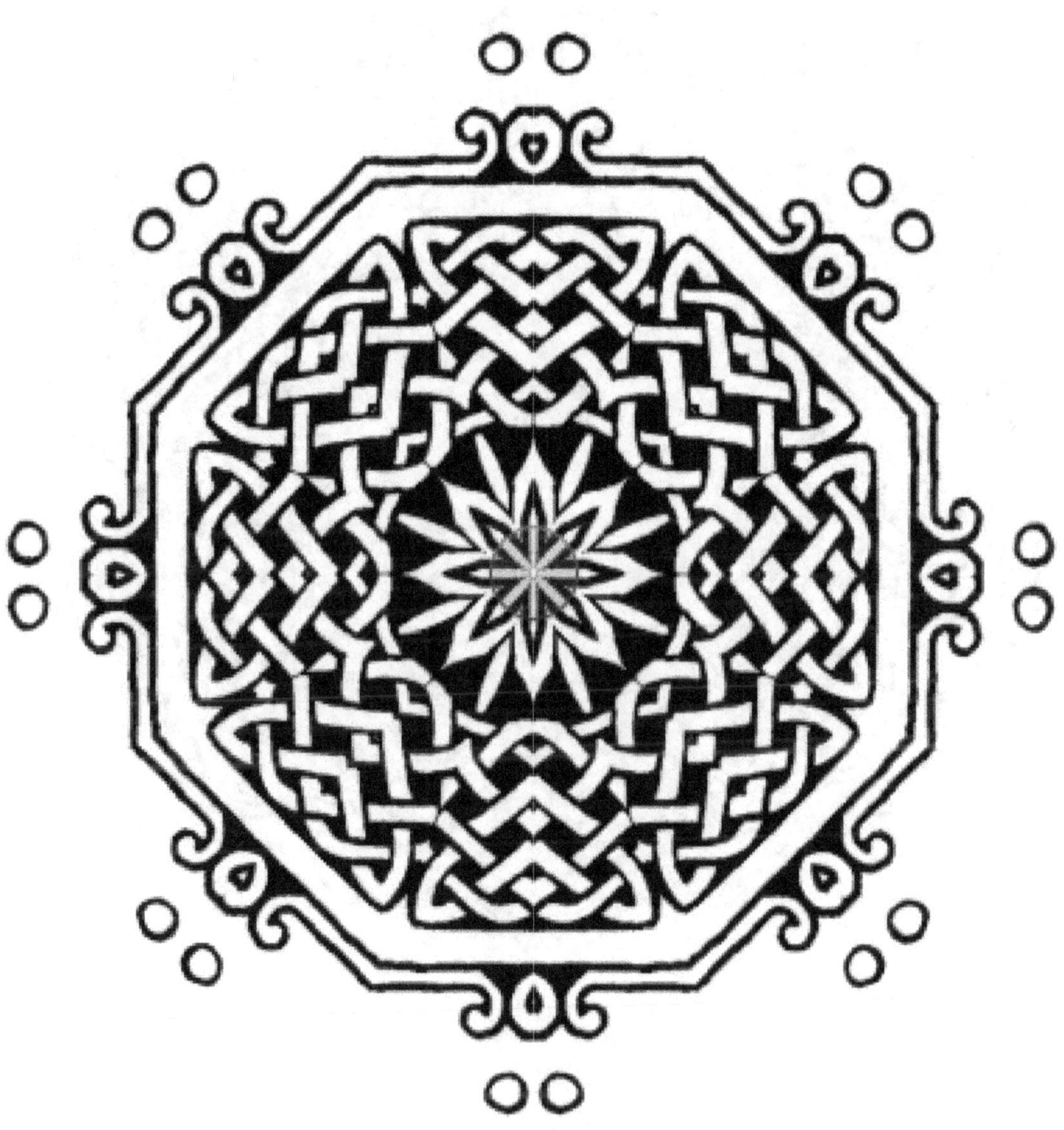

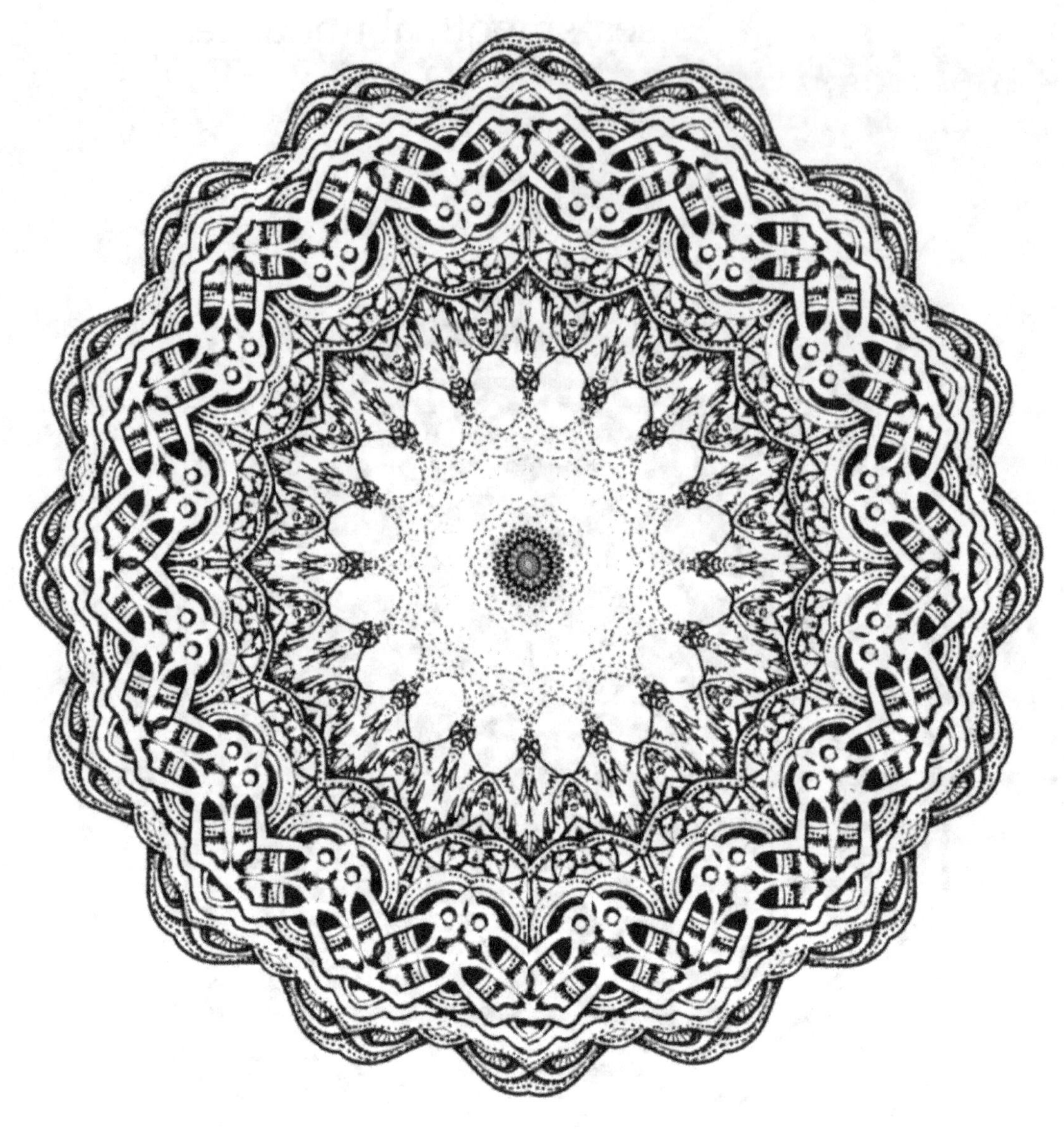

My eyes bathed in love,
there is always only You
to turn to, Meher.

Keep smiling at me,
Beloved, please. It keeps me
hanging on Your line.

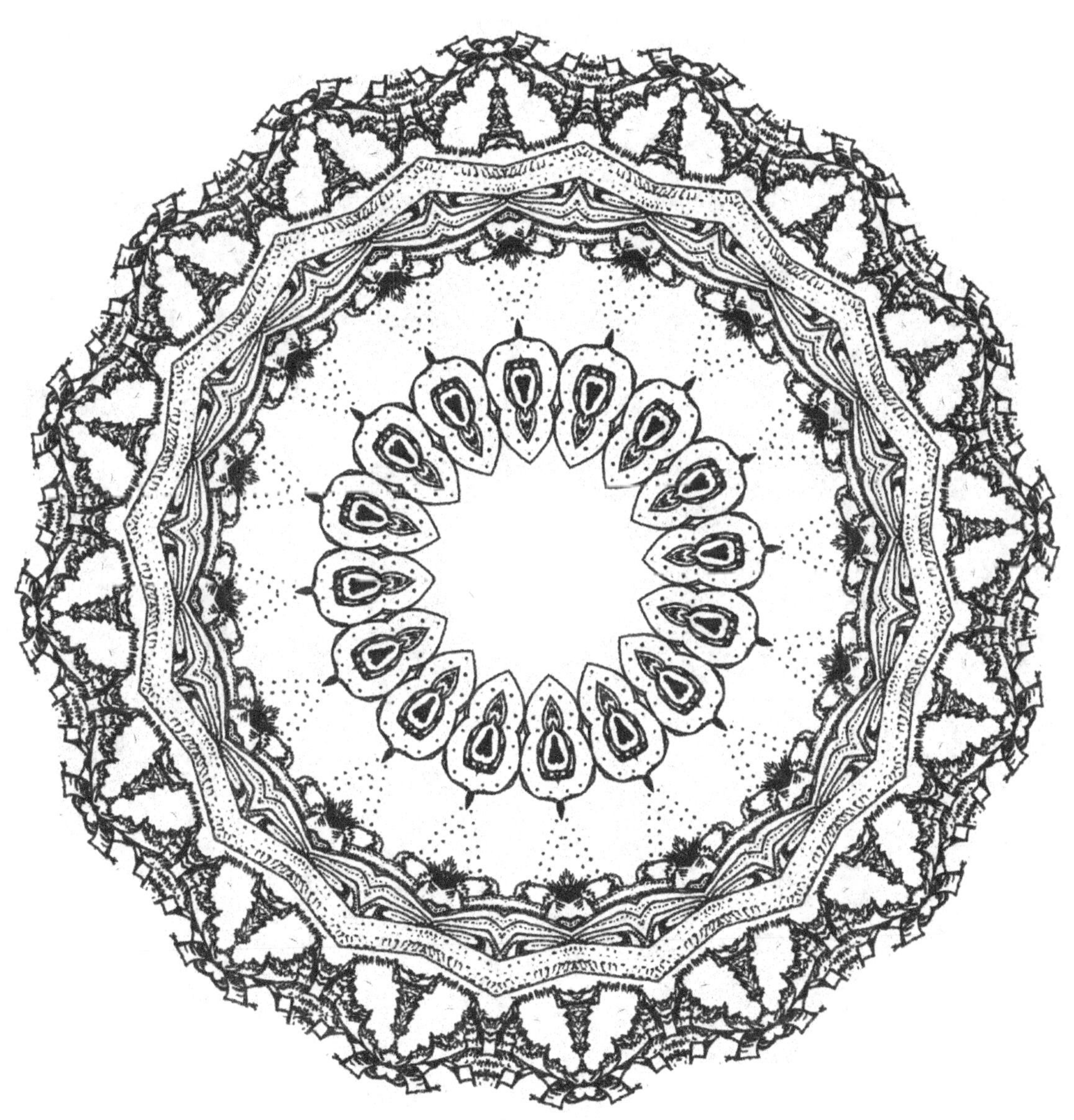

I know You know me —
that helps to remember — one
day I will know You!

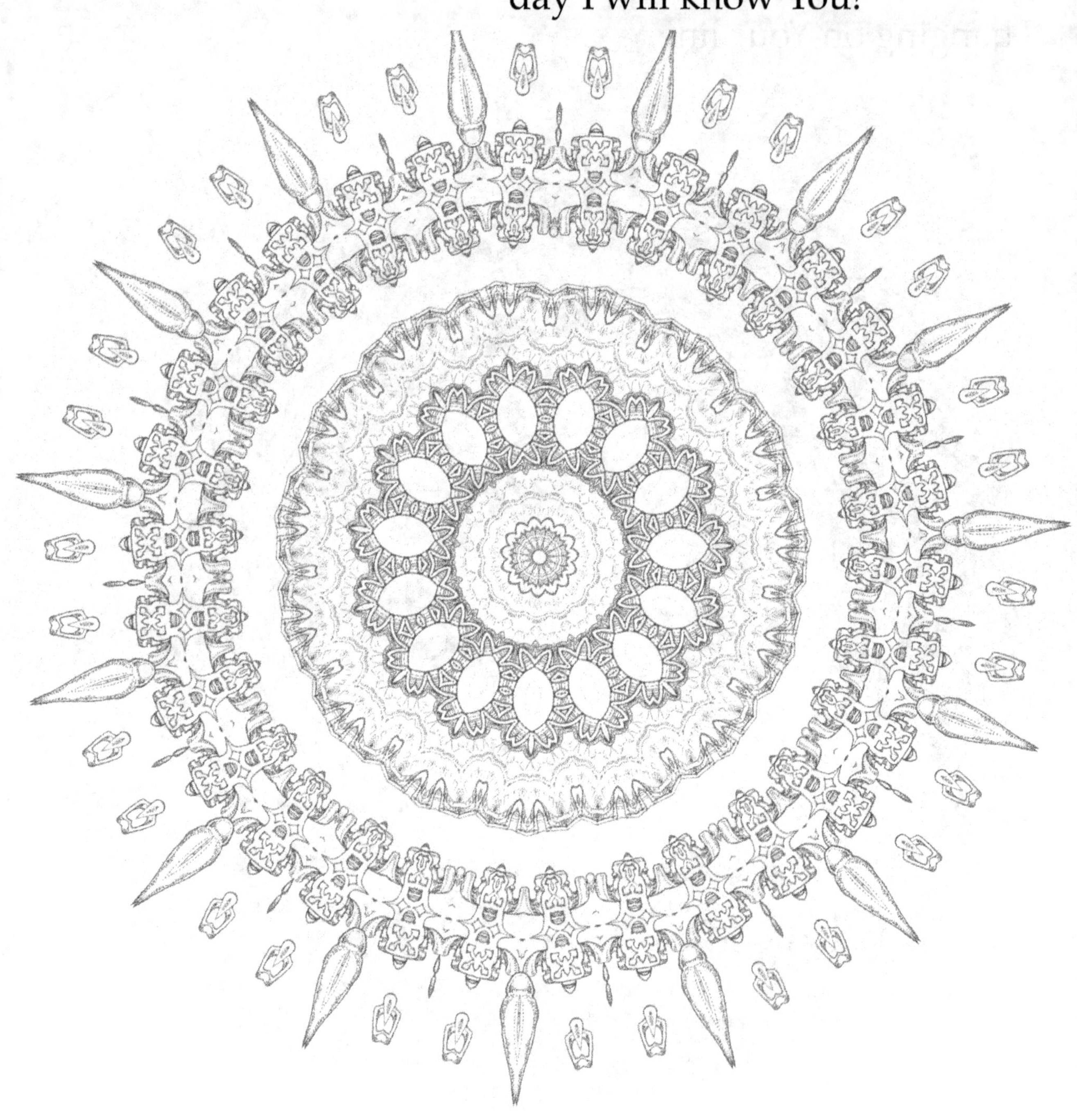

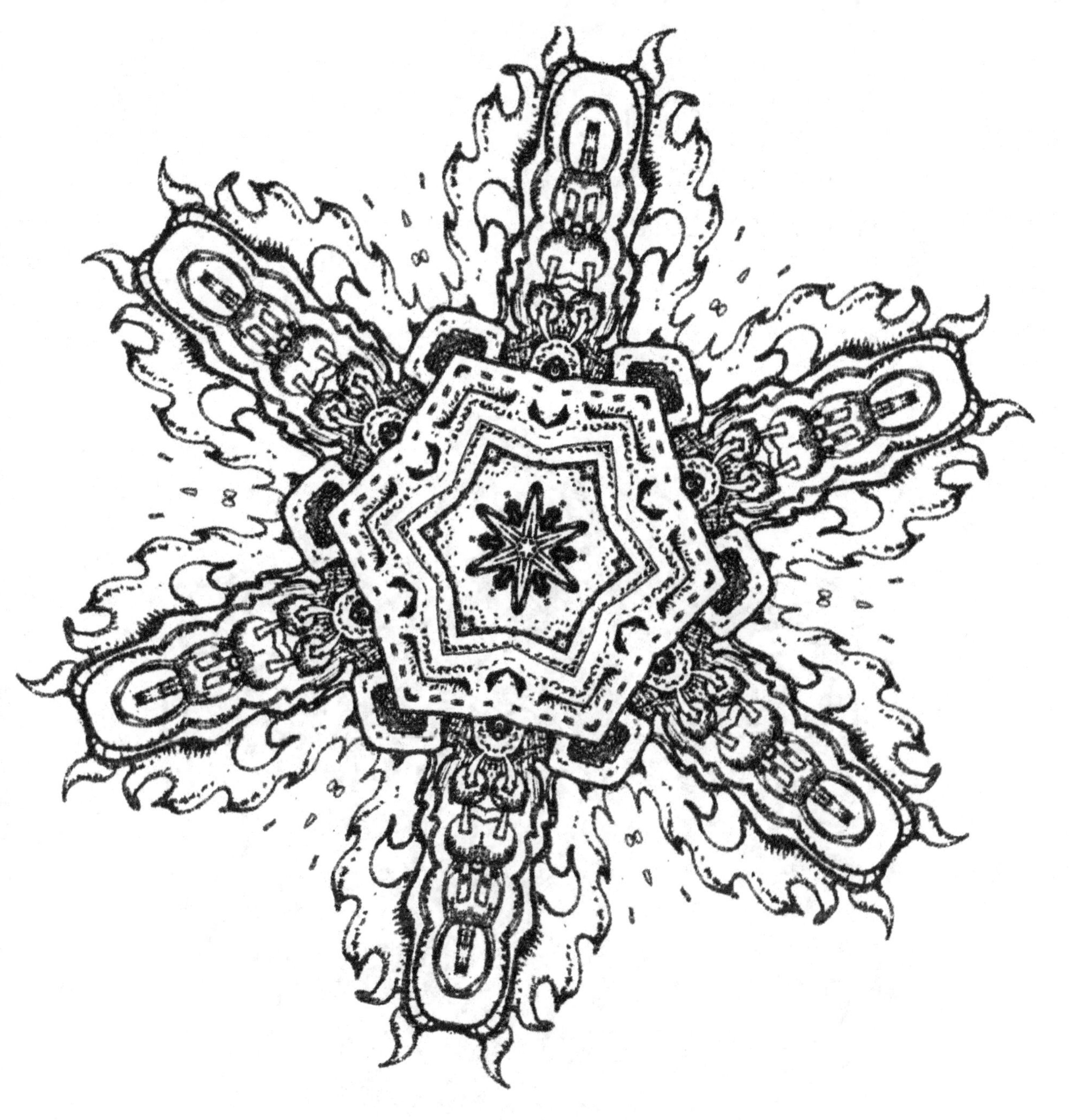

Mine is now to walk
up the quiet tree-lined path,
burning off the night.

You — the Voice of Calm,
You again, to point the Way —
this Way, *come to Love*.

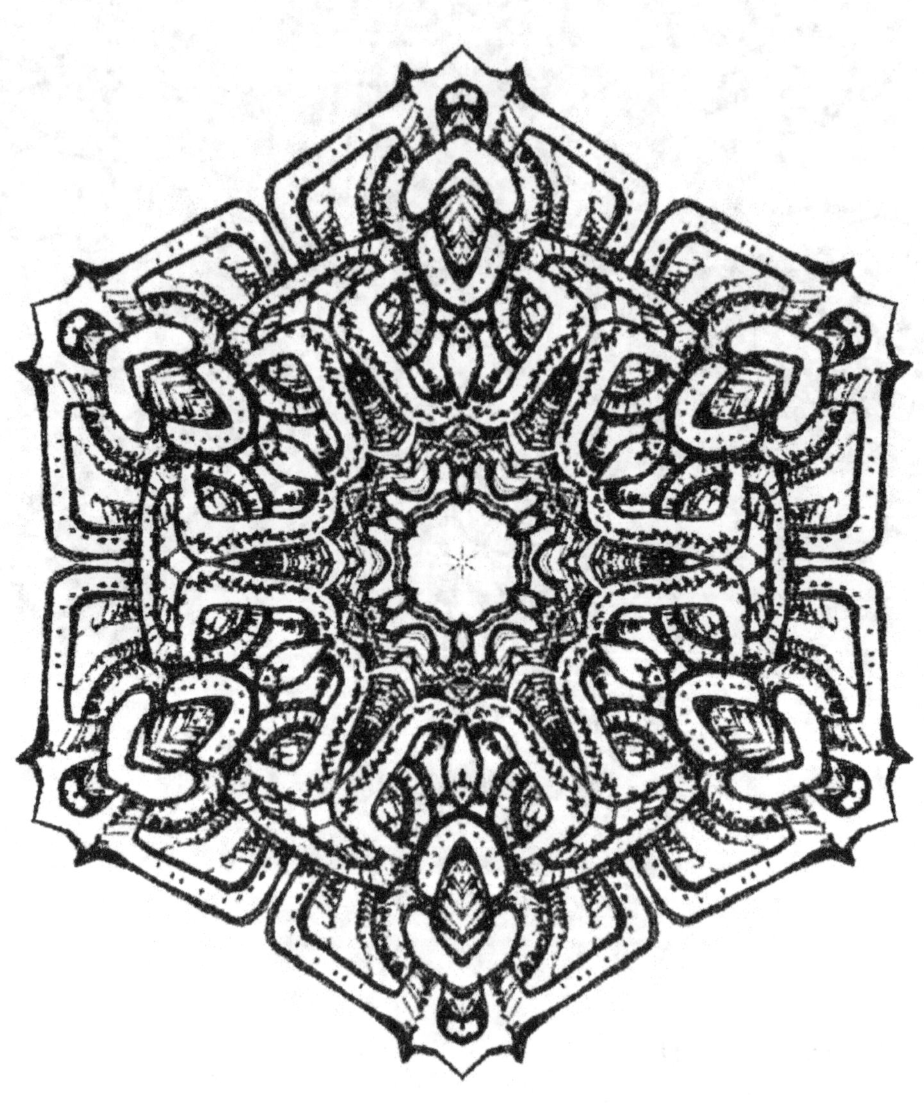

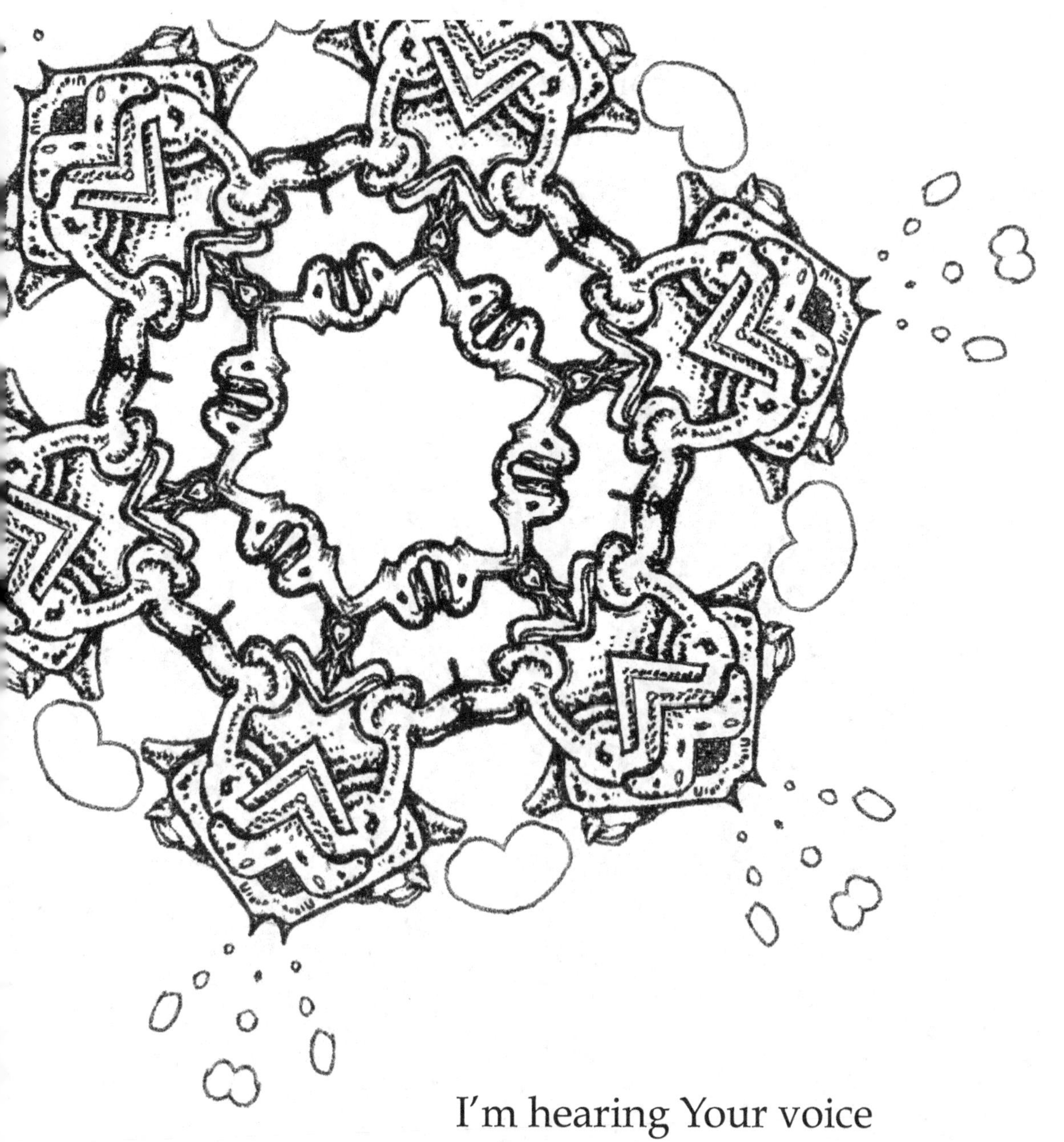

I'm hearing Your voice
differently now — it's a
breeze from paradise.

The trail follows you
moment by moment, He says,
blessing every step.

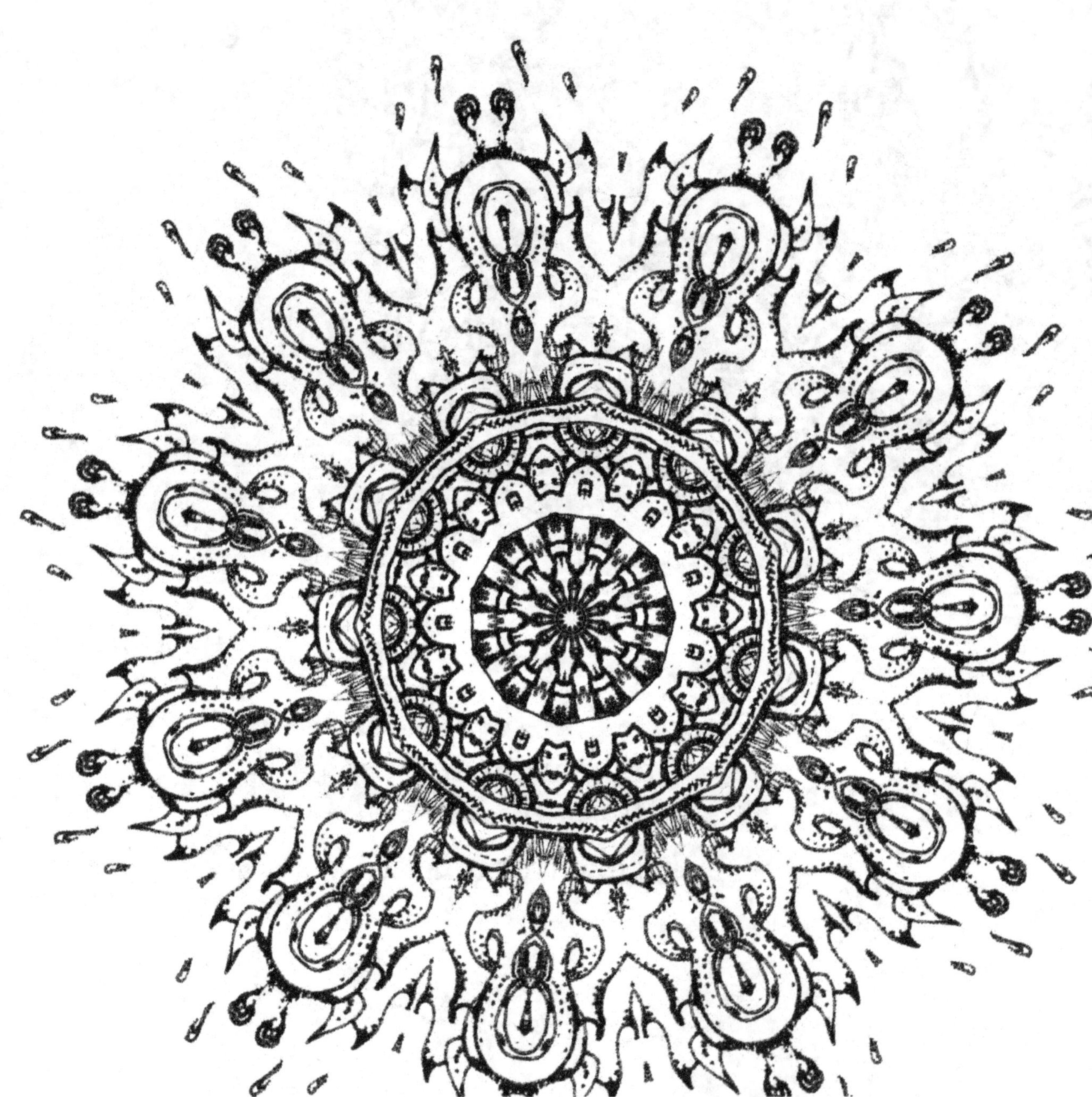

You *are* the sparkle,
the sunshot gur-gurgling stream—
one rushing danceflow.

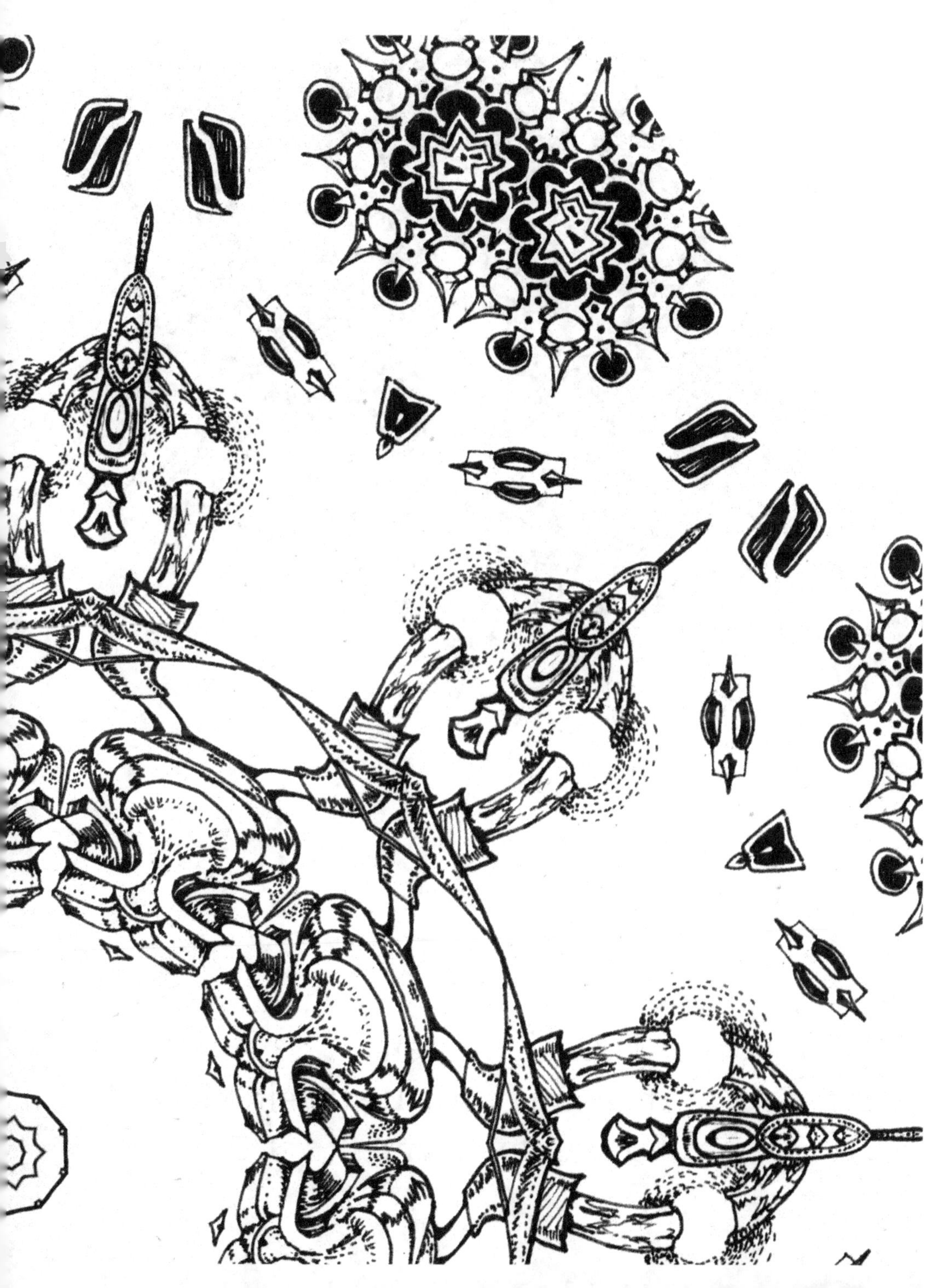

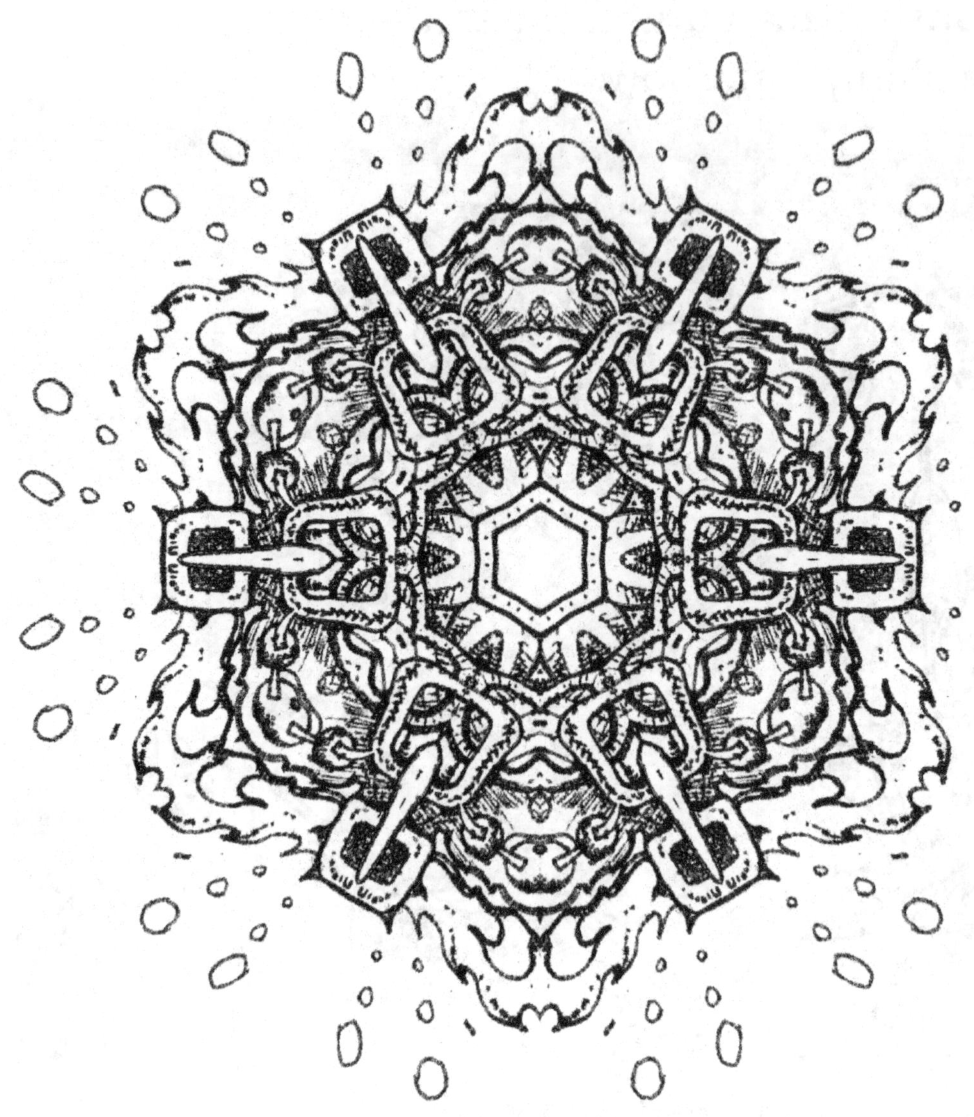

I unpack hidden
treasure of my Real Self—Love,
Love enlivens me.

Love notes, like droplets
of spring rain falling from leaves,
awaken my heart.

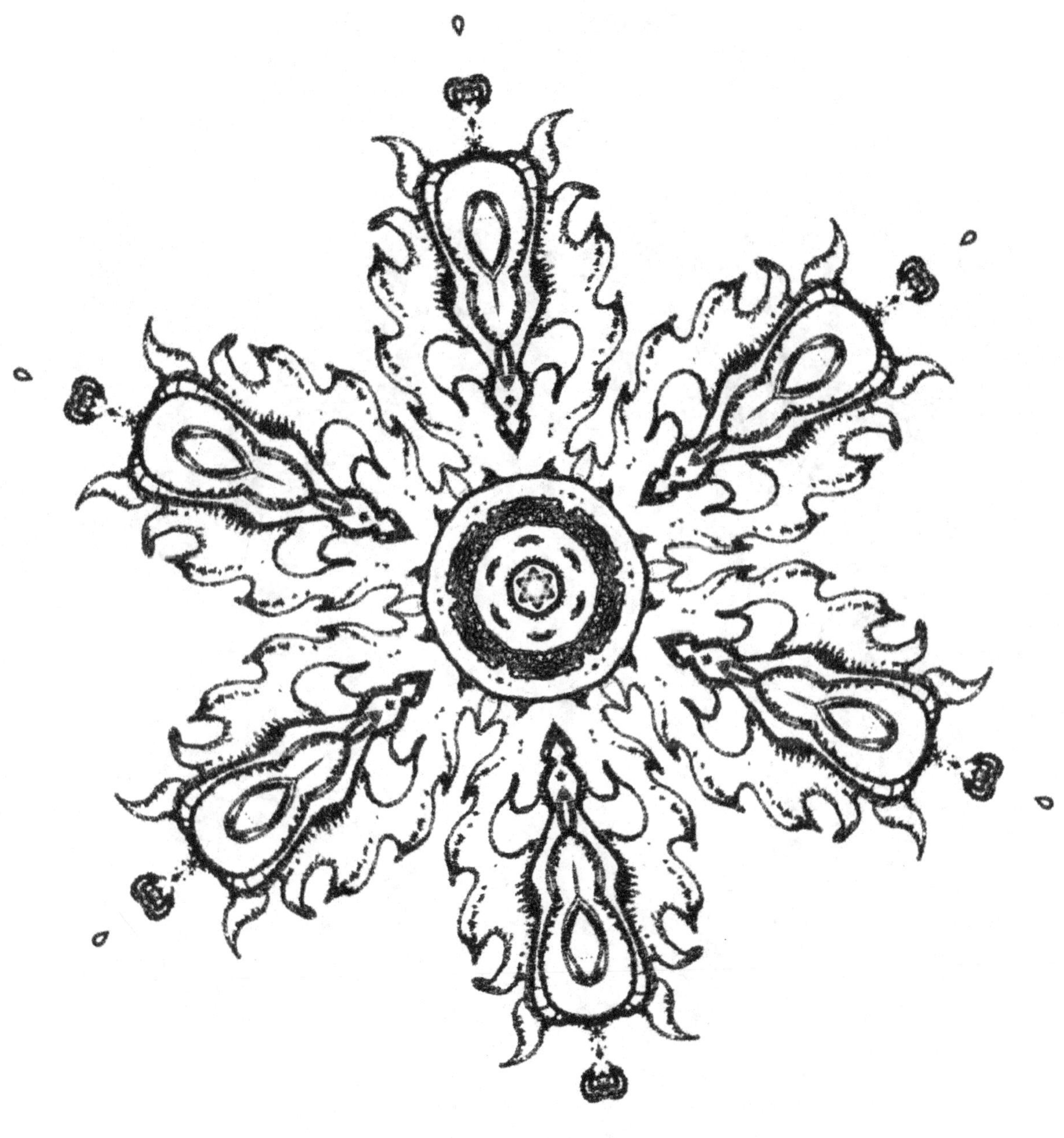

Content in the state
of not knowing, I trust Your
guidance within me.

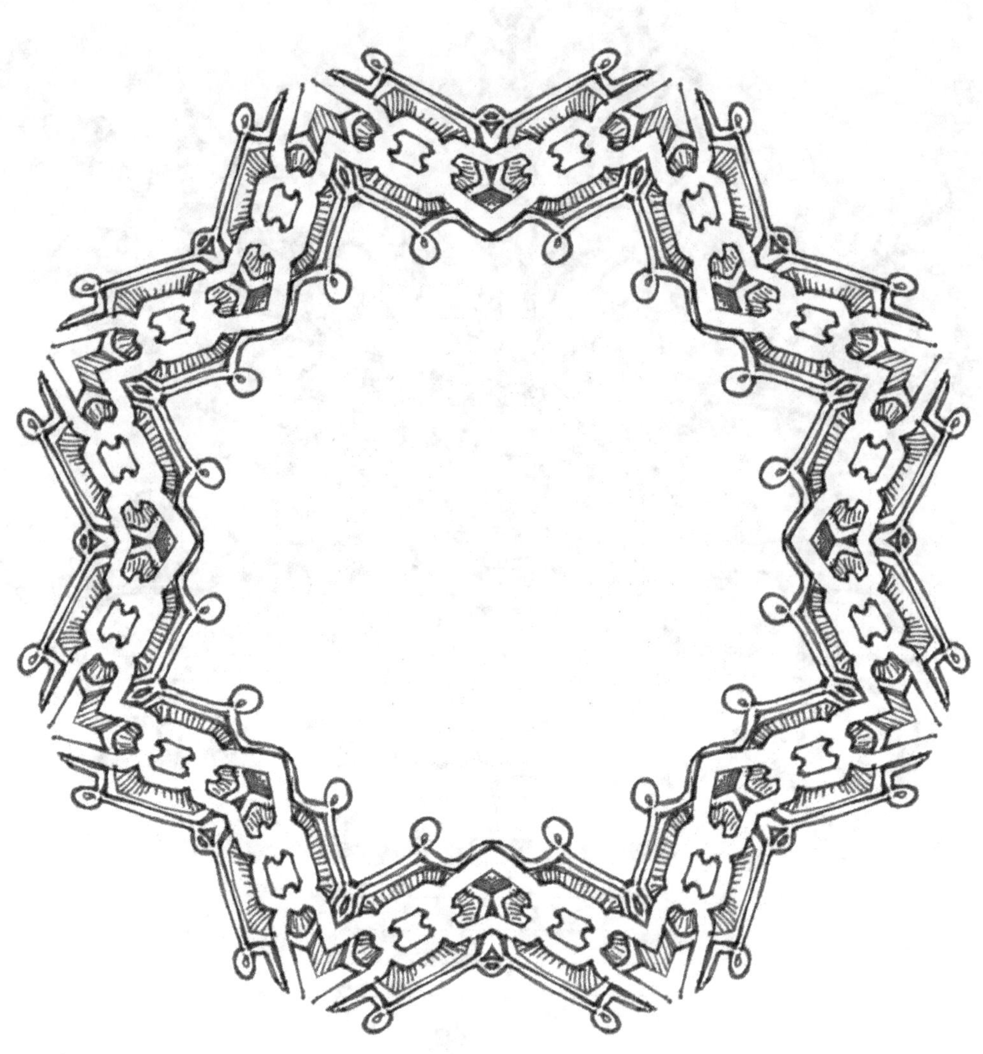

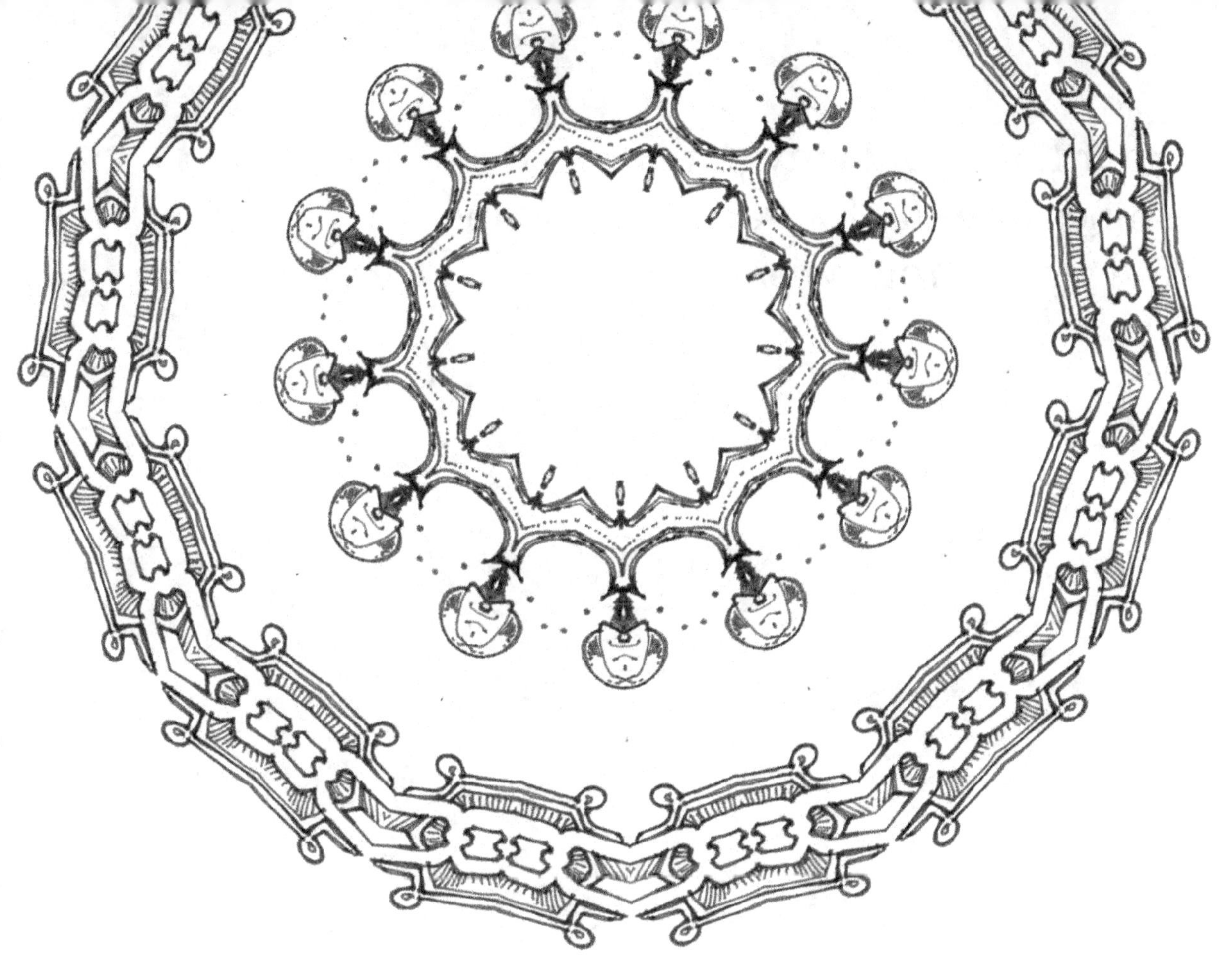

A new perspective
shows the heart of another
to my opened eye.

Your Love lights my path,
shines brightly forward — shows me
the way to Your wish.

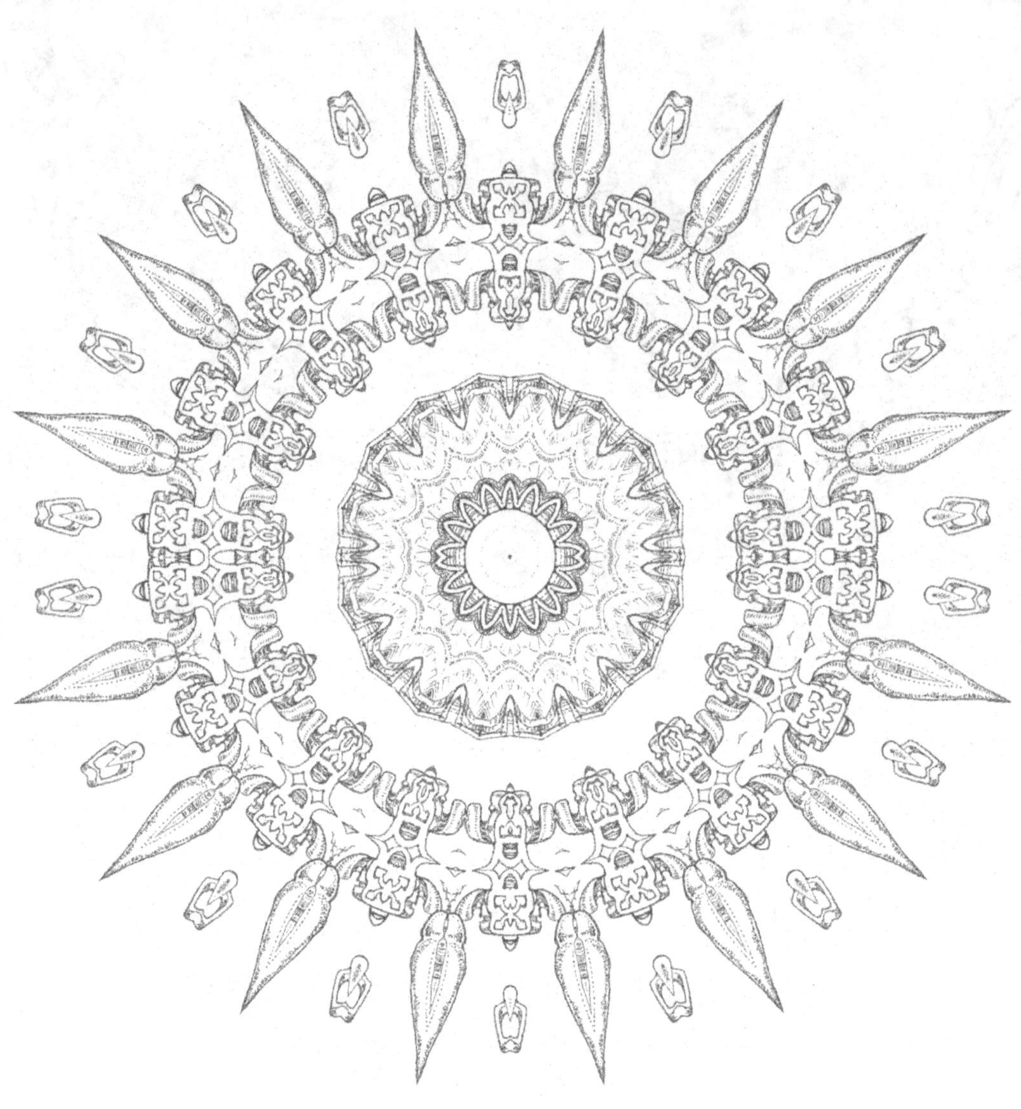

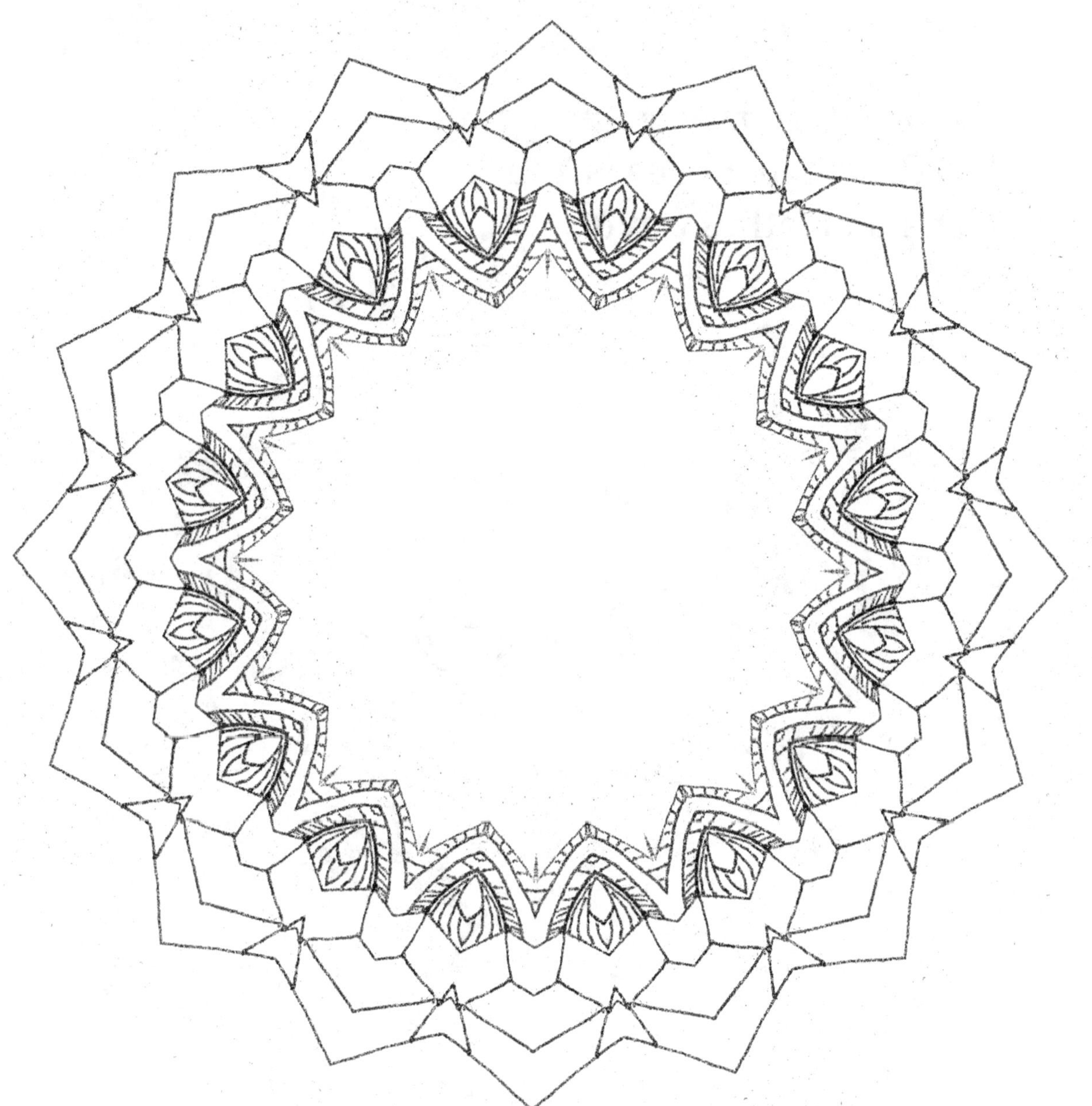

Let's open our hearts—
invite Him to turn the key—
one Ocean for all.

She breathes prayer upon prayer.
The Rose in her eyes is You.
Mehera breathes Love.

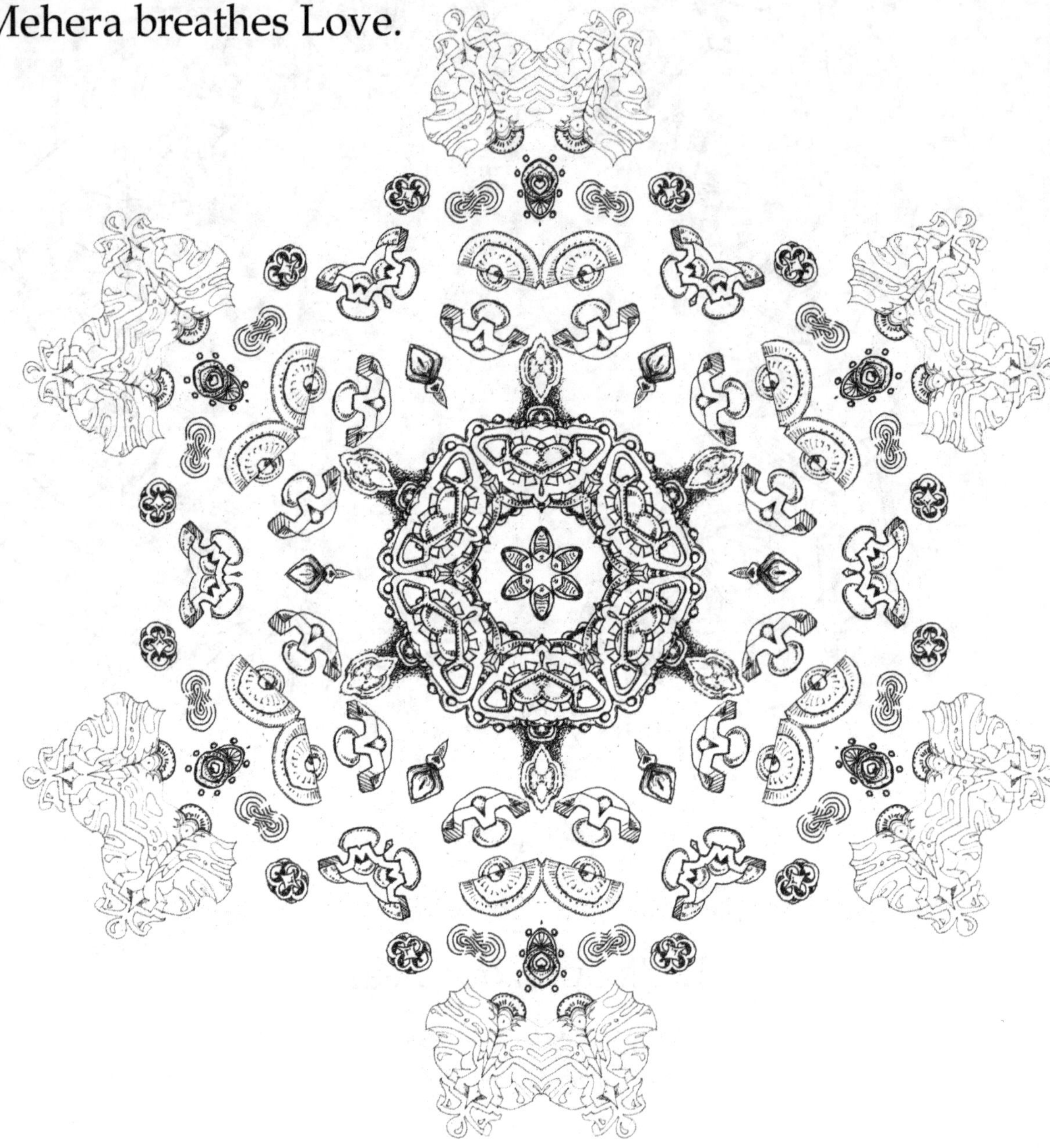

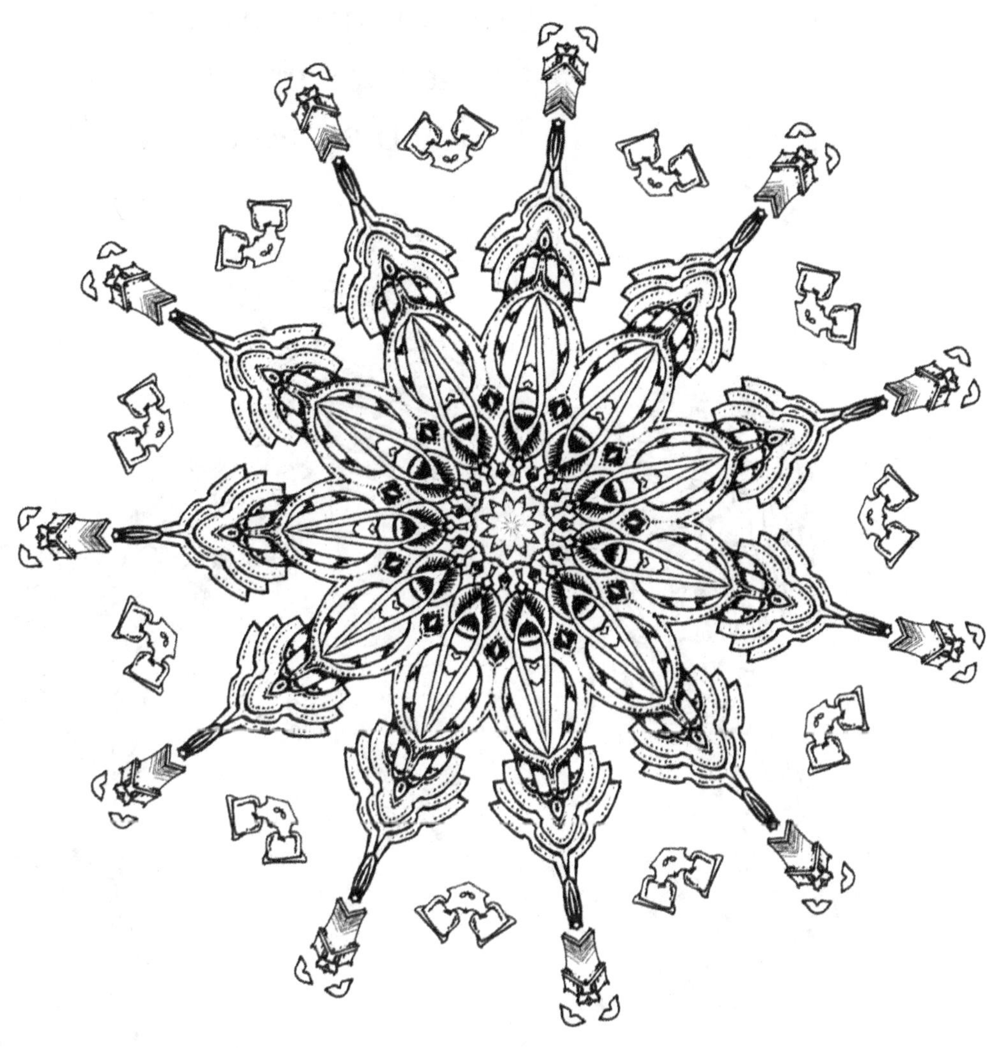

When things don't line up,
there is something squiggling behind
what seems obvious.

Sun shining on me.
Raindrops gentle down on me.
Twice blessed as I walk.

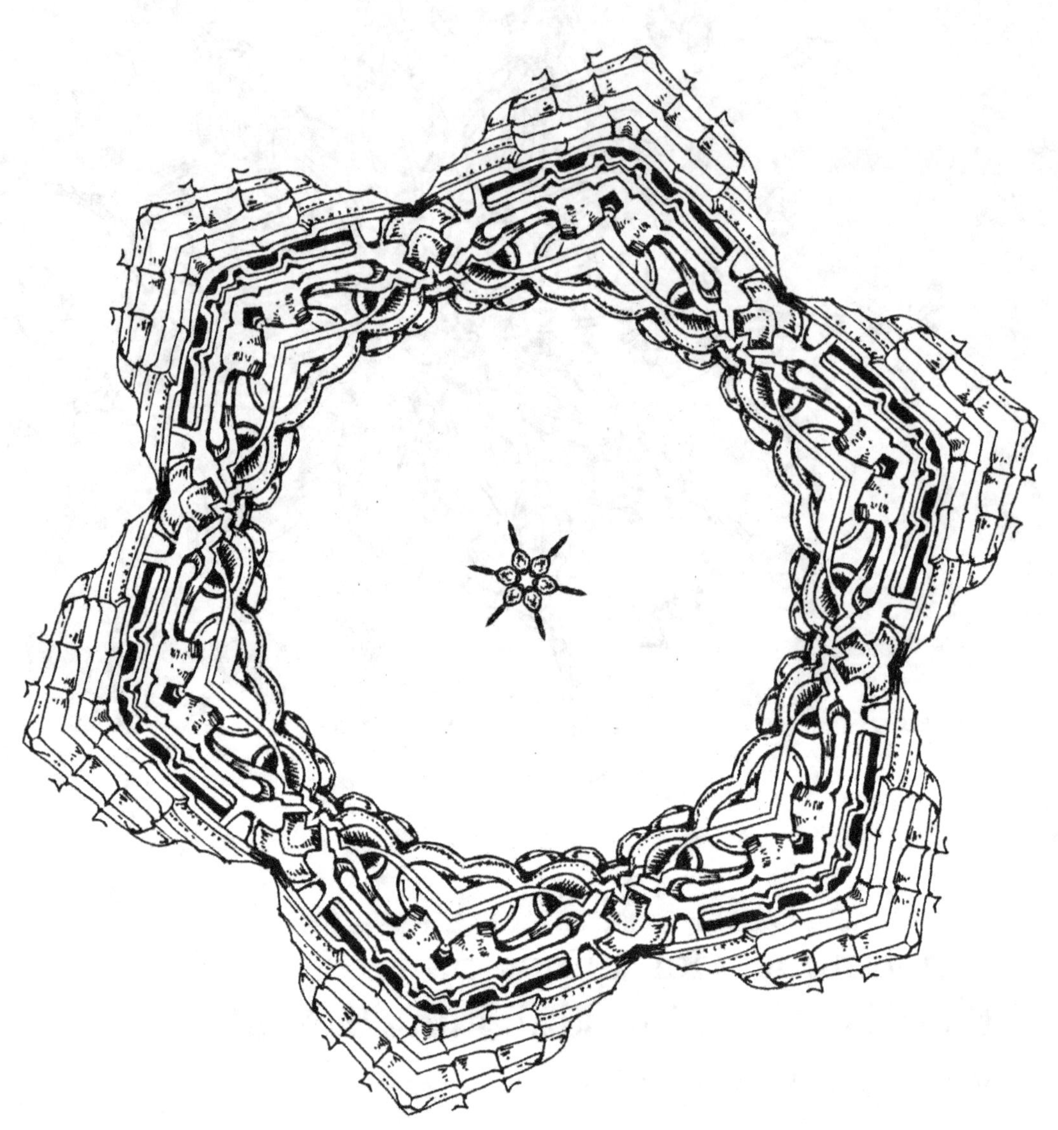

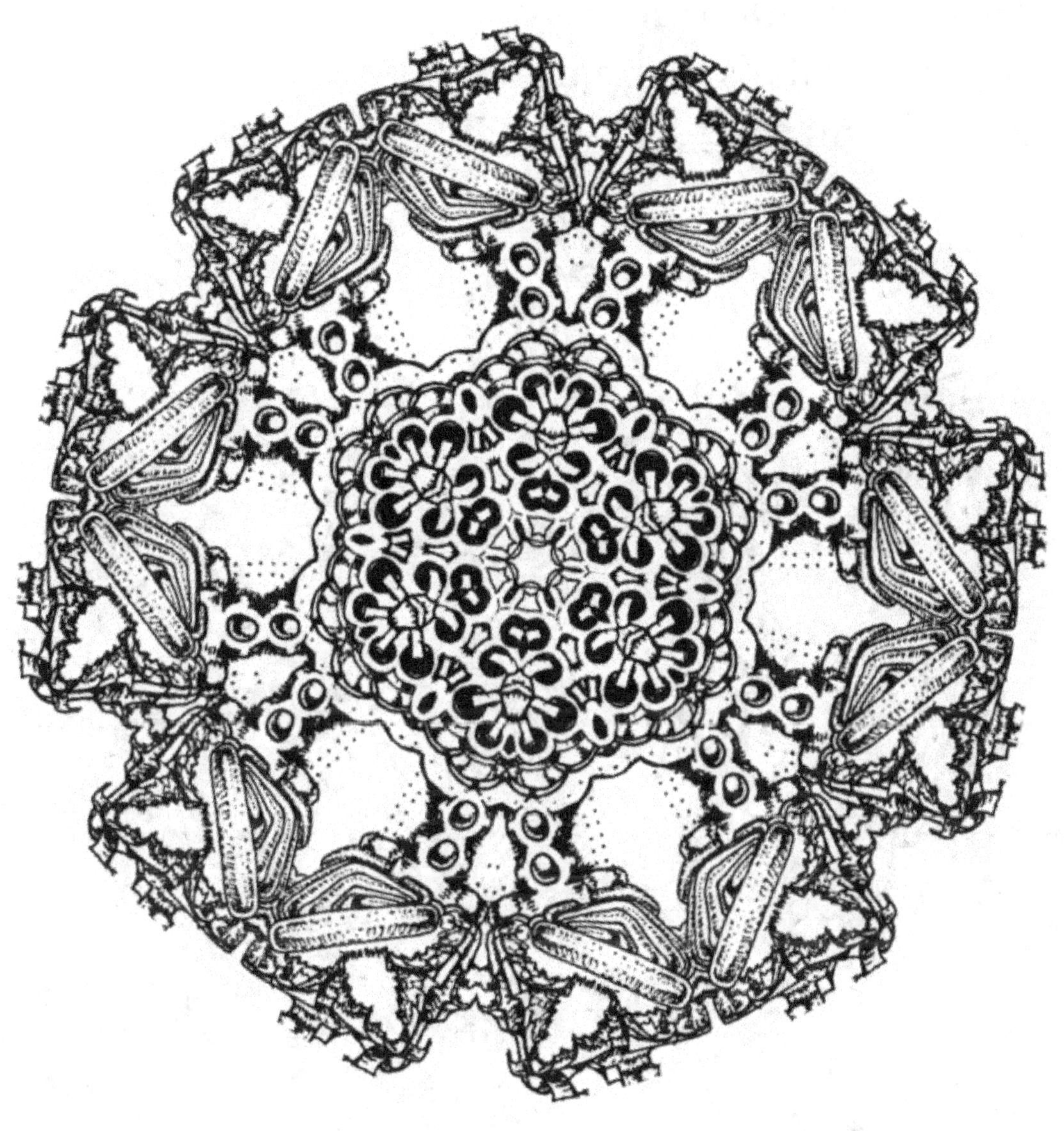

I no longer need
the blackness of cats and crows —
take Death as a lover!

Hitch a wild wild ride,
hang on to Baba's daaman—
head to Rumi's field!

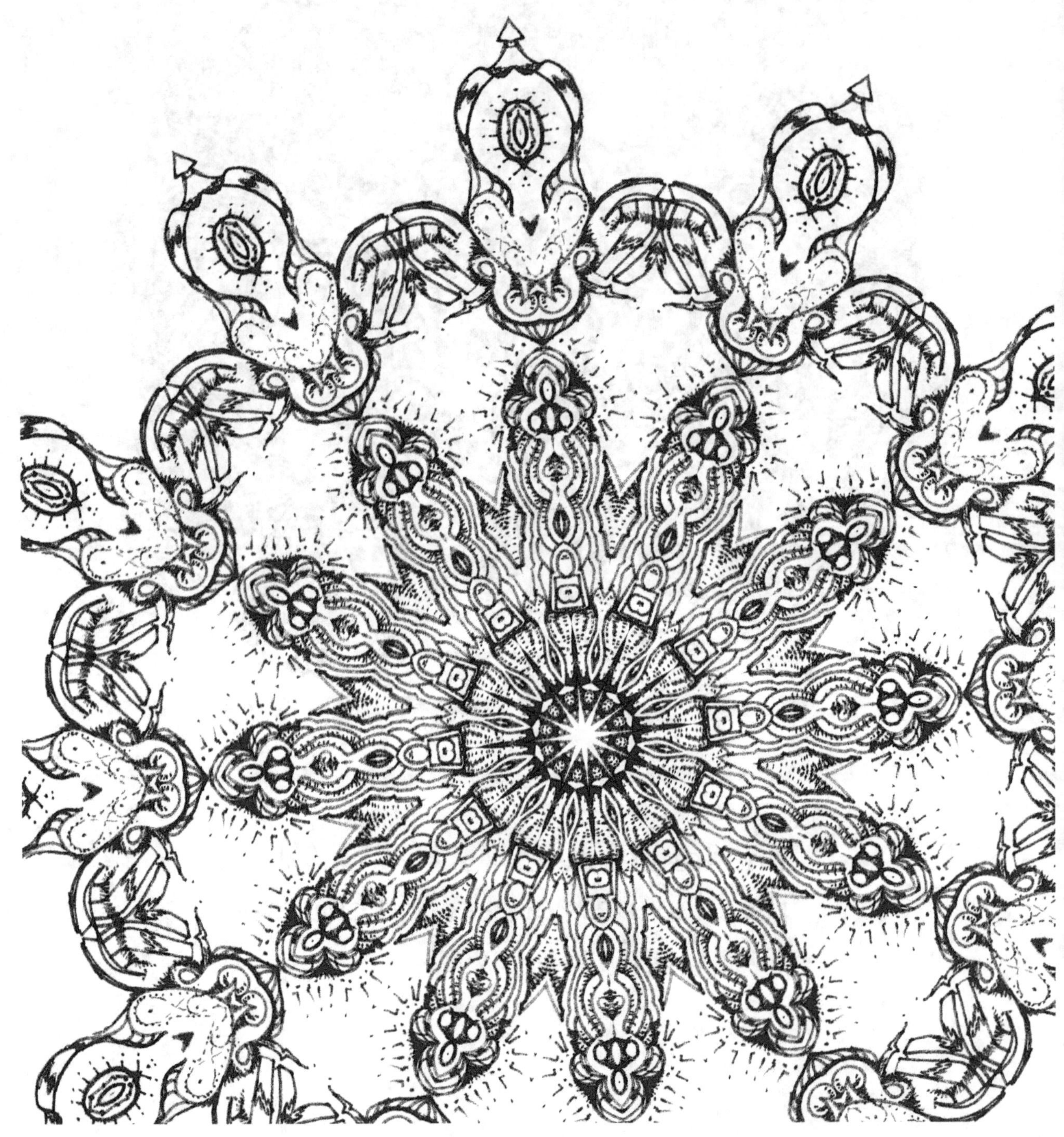

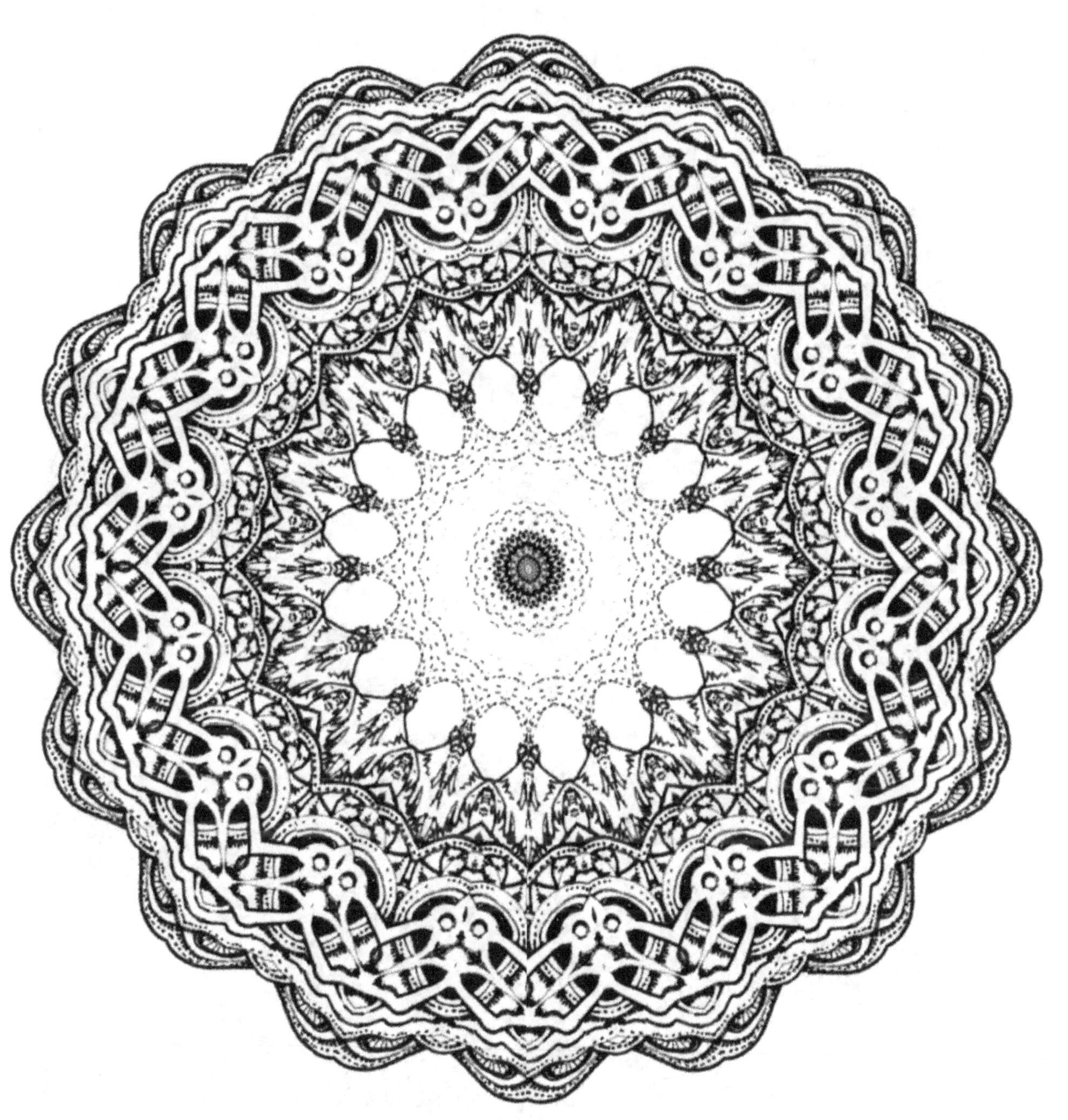

I just want to play
in Rumi's field, unfettered
and silent, with You.

Summer walls of green
along every road we take—
hills, valleys of green!

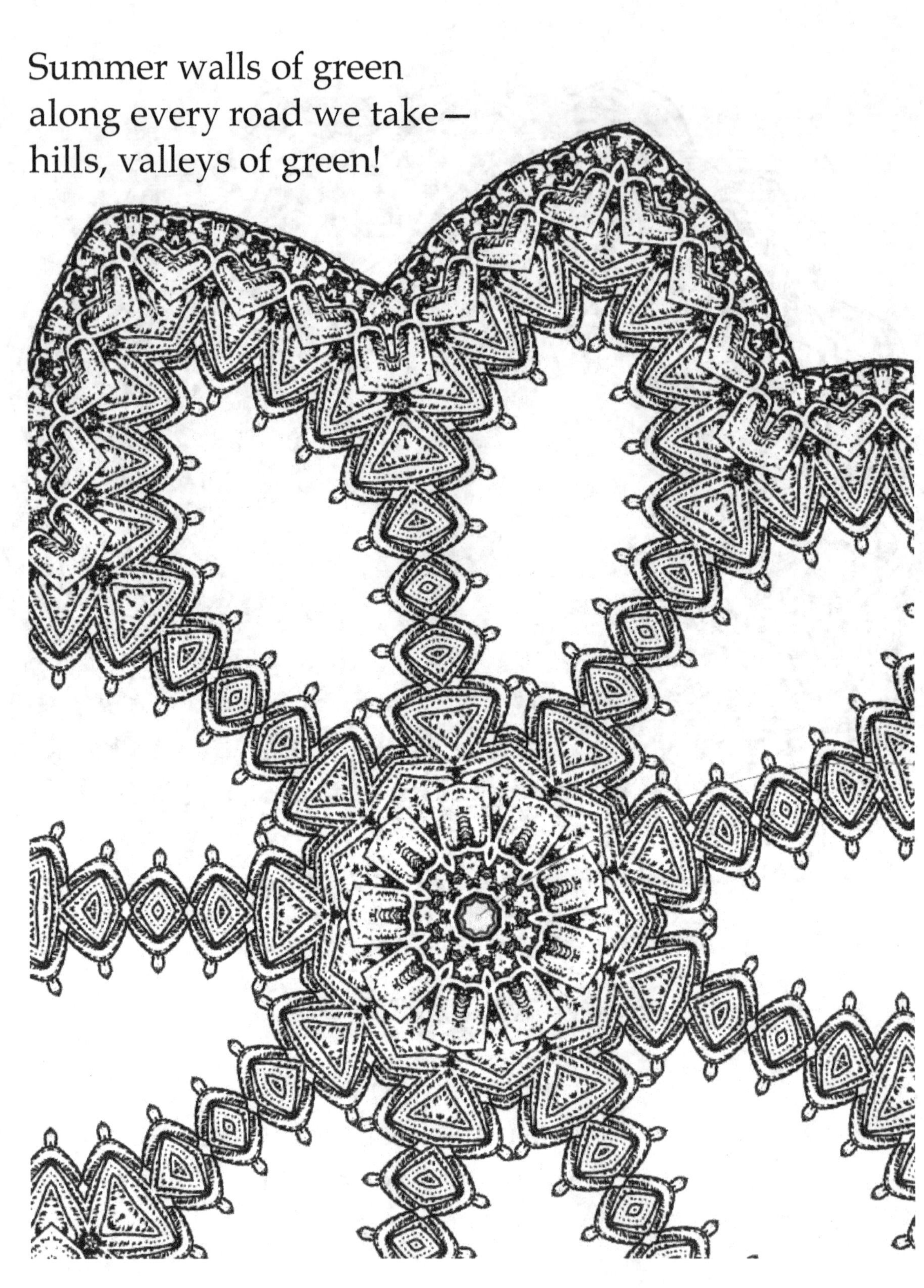

Big armfuls of light,
a basketful of rising suns
burning off the night.

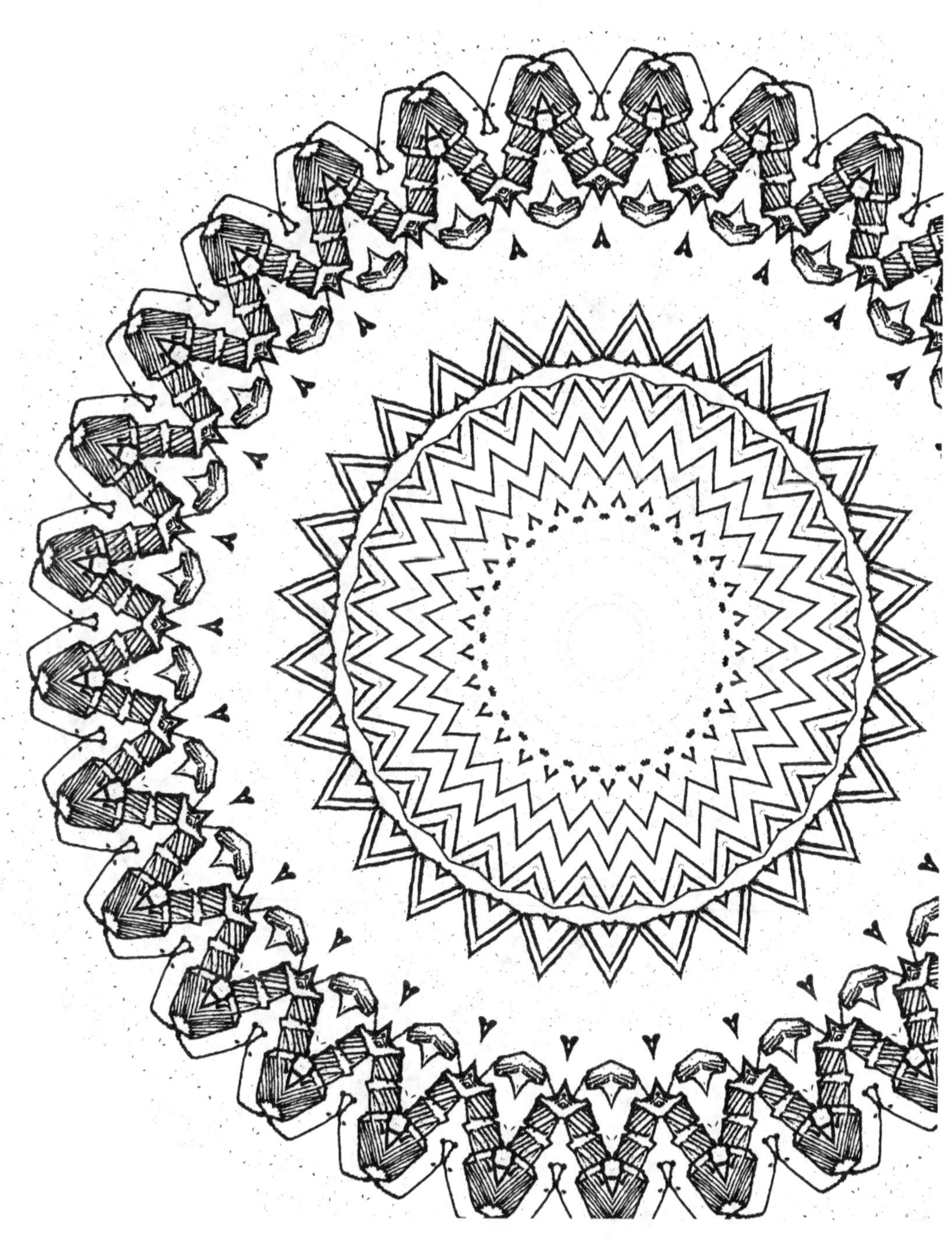

Dark Horse

Coming from behind—
fast and faster—headed for
Your Love, O Meher!

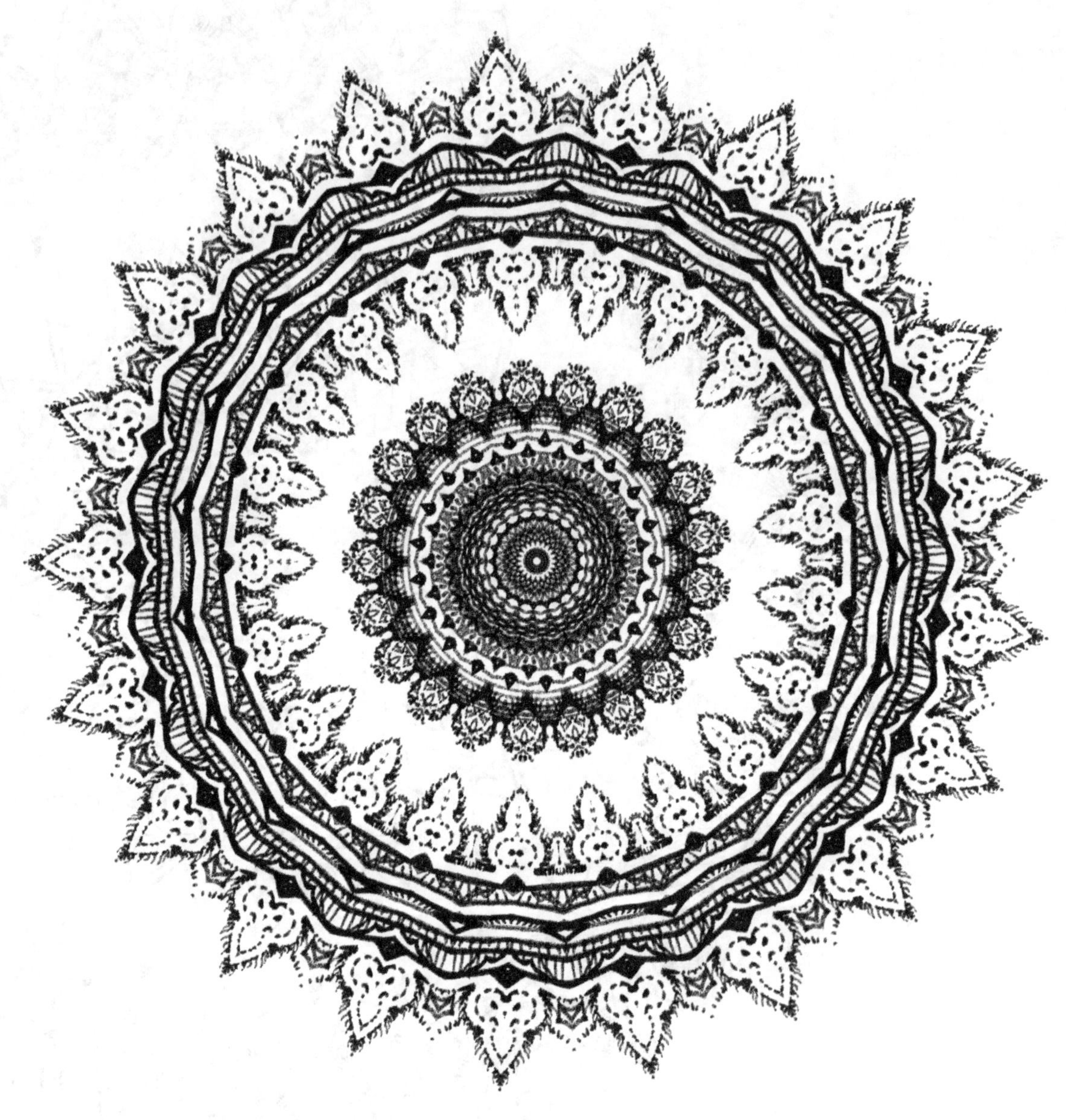